Northern Ireland, Scotland & Wales

Edited by Donna Samworth

 Young**Writers**

First published in Great Britain in 2008 by:
Young Writers
Remus House
Coltsfoot Drive
Peterborough
PE2 9JX
Telephone: 01733 890066
Website: www.youngwriters.co.uk

SB ISBN 978-1 84431 502 4

Foreword

Young Writers was established in 1991 and has been passionately devoted to the promotion of reading and writing in children and young adults ever since. The quest continues today. Young Writers remains as committed to the nurturing of poetic and literary talent as ever.

This year's Young Writers competition has proven as vibrant and dynamic as ever and we are delighted to present a showcase of the best poetry from across the UK and in some cases overseas. Each poem has been selected from a wealth of *Little Laureates* entries before ultimately being published in this, our sixteenth primary school poetry series.

Once again, we have been supremely impressed by the overall quality of the entries we have received. The imagination, energy and creativity which has gone into each young writer's entry made choosing the poems a challenging and often difficult but ultimately hugely rewarding task - the general high standard of the work submitted ensured this opportunity to bring their poetry to a larger appreciative audience.

We sincerely hope you are pleased with this final collection and that you will enjoy *Little Laureates Northern Ireland, Scotland & Wales* for many years to come.

Contents

Jessica Rosser (8)	14
Joshua Rhys Thomas & Ieuan David Stradling (9)	15
Amy Davies & Caroline Millan (8)	15
Joseph Cornwall (8) & Katherine Thompson	15
Aaron James Harvey (8)	16
Lewis Mainwaring (8)	16
Caitlin Morgan (8)	16
Ellie Lewis & Sam Freeman (8)	17
Caroline Millan & Amy Davies (8)	17
Zoe Dowling (8)	17
Cameron Dobbs, Liam Griffiths (7), Liam Goodall, Justin Hearn (8), Jessica Moule, Niome Andrews, Rebecca Ellis, Mathew Watkins & Liam Miles (10)	18
Benjamin Powell (9)	18
Ffion Williams (9)	19
Rhys Chapman (8)	19
Bethan Mulligan (9)	20
Louis Evans (9)	20
Rhys Austin (9)	21
Nia Parry-Howells (10)	21
Dylan Matthews (9)	22
Ellie Plumb-Darrell (9)	22
Connor Jones (9)	23
Natalie Jones (9)	23
Eleanor Collins (10)	24
Robyn Tucker (9)	24
Tamara Jones (9)	24
Robert Curtis (9)	25

Brynmenyn Primary School, Bridgend

Charlotte Thomas (9)	25
Elle Edwards (7)	25
Daniel Elward (8)	26
Shane Hill (9)	26
Floyd Panizales (8)	26
Lucy Morgan (8)	27
Bethan Thomas (7)	27
Cohan Lewis (9)	27
Katie Ellis (9)	28
Loren Bennett (8)	28
Nia Gronow (9)	29

Keiran Herbert (9)   29
Daisy Faulkner (8)   30
Lily Ile (7)   30
Grace Ellis (7)   30
Shauna Griffiths (9)   31
Ben Page (9)   31
Brook Lewis (7)   31
Rachel Randall (8)   32
Joseph Williams (9)   32
Adam Cooke (9)   33
Bradley Newman (7)   33

Cookstown Primary School, Cookstown
Megan Reid (8)   34
Jamie Lindsay (10)   34
Jessica Stewart (8)   34
Joshua Glendinning (7)   35
Megan McCrea (7)   35
Tia Warnock (7)   35
Danny Kerr (7)   36
Curtis Hodgett (8)   36
Lois Cooke (8)   37
Claudia Wylie (7)   37
Shantel Shannon (7)   38
Olivia Woods (7)   38
Matthew Crooks (7)   38
Steven Arrell (8)   39
Nathen Espie (7)   39
Daniel Stewart (8)   39
Hannah Mowbray (7)   40
Thomas Simpson (7)   40
Joel Loughrin (8)   41
Amy Carson (8)   41
Matthew Young (7)   42
Ryan Wilkinson (8)   42
Jack Dingley (8)   42
Sam Ferguson (7)   43
Matthew Ruck (7)   43
Andrea Boyle (8)   43
Grace Gilmore (7)   44
Bethany Stoker (7)   44

Vincent Wong (7)	45
Jordan Scott (7)	45
Chloe Brownlow (7)	46
Emily Slaine (8)	46
Ellie May Parke (7)	47
Lauren Henry (8)	47
Sarah Dorothea Wilson (7)	48
Grace Miller (8)	48
Lois Glendinning (8)	49
Chloe McGuigan (7)	49
Marc Glasgow (7)	50
Shalanda Shannon (7)	50
Leah Anderson (8)	51
Sam Purvis (8)	51
Adam Martin (8)	52
Cameron Mullan (8)	52

Crosshouse Primary School, East Kilbride

Tommy Kilpatrick (10)	53
Kirsten Macaulay (10	53
Ian Lonsdale (10)	54
Tegan Brodie (9)	54
Caitlin Abberley (10)	54
Chloe Kennedy (10)	55
Louise McFarlane (10)	55
Jack Reid (10)	55
Conor Smith (10)	56
Paige Matthews (10)	56
Shaun McCann (9)	57

Cwmclydach Primary School, Tonypandy

Jessica Lam (10)	57
Curtis Povey (10)	58
Henry Murphy (9)	58
Anna-Rose Thomas (10)	59
Jonathan Thomas (9)	59
Kieran Thomas (10)	60
Lewis Thomas (9)	60
Matthew Parsons (10)	61
Kyran Thomas (9)	61
Simone Thomas (10)	62

Nikita McCarthay (10)	62
Devon Howard (10)	63
Corey Thomas (10)	63
Adam Monaghan (11)	64
Shannon Webber (10)	64
Rhys Thomas (10)	65
Adrian Gerald Griffiths	65
Josh Edwards (10)	66
Chloe Edwards (9)	66
Joel Shanley Davies (10)	67
Corie Southwood (11)	67

Evish Primary School, Strabane

Rian McDaid (10)	68
Ryan Flanagan (11)	68
Aoife Devine (10)	69
Seaghda Cullen (9)	69

Godre'rgraig Primary School, Godre'rgraig

Emily Davies (11)	70
Eben Vaughan-Philipps (9)	71
Lucy Griffiths (10)	72
Joshua Hopkin (11)	73
Emilia Lawrence (10)	74
Aimee Lauren Jones (10)	75
Liam James Walsh (10)	76
Jo Diana Price (10)	77
Chlöe Hughes (9)	78
Suzie Chang (10)	79
Georgia May Meyrick (10)	80
Elisha Flack (10)	81
Abigail Zoe Jones (9)	82
Jessica Amber Danaher (9)	83
Ashley Clavey (11)	84
Carys Phillips (9)	85
Tamzin Diaper (9)	86
Lauren Jones (9)	86
Kasey-Jayne Counsell (10)	87

Gortin Primary School, Gortin

Naomi McConnell (9)   88
Aaron McMullin (7)   88
Alex Hempton (8)   89
Scott McNally (7)   89
Jacob McIlwaine (9)   90
Andrew McFarland (9)   90
Thomas McIlwaine (8)   90
Chloe Campbell (10)   91
Emily Pinkerton (9)   91
Zara Donnell (10)   91
Aimee Porter (9)   92
Joshua Godber (10)   92
Nadine Kilpatrick (10)   92

Greenhills Primary School, Glasgow

Jade Burns (9)   93
James McCann (10)   93

Kildrum Primary School, Cumbernauld

Ryan Auld (10)   94
Declan Cameron Murphy (10)   94
Cameron McTavish (9)   95
Sarah Louise Bergin (10)   95
Kayleigh Armstrong (9)   96
Sarah Thornton (9)   96
Michael Mallinder-Macleod (10)   96
Rebekah L Lindsay (10)   97
Andrew King (10)   97
Darren Aitken (10)   97
Misha Davidson (10)   98
Alan Symington (10)   98
Sean Mendelovitch (10)   98
Stuart Boyce (10)   99
Antonia Brodie (10)   99

Llanedeyrn Primary School, Llanedeyrn

Daniel Thomas (10)   100
Callum Jennings   100

Adele O'Sullivan (10)   101
Farid Rashid (10)   101

Miltonbank Primary School, Glasgow
Callum Forrester (11)   102

Our Lady of the Angels RC School, Old Cwmbran
Morgan Thomas (8)   102
Elizabeth Earthey (9)   103
Lily Rafter Ambrosen (7)   103
Jacob McMorrow (10)   104
Huw Powell (9)   104
Christiana Sturch (10)   105
Bethany Smith (9)   105

St Brigid's Primary School, Cranagh
Ann McGarvey (9)   106
Michael McMullan (8)   106
Stephen McGarvey (8)   106
Orla Kennedy (8)   107
Emma McCullagh (9)   107
Owen Conway (10)   107
Hannah McMullan (9)   108
Brónach Falls (8)   108
Leanne McCrory (8)   109
Kelly McMullan (11)   109
Roisin McAneney (9)   110
Aine Bradley (8)   110
Eunan Conway (8)   110

St Catherine's Primary School, Glasgow
Eve Taylor-Fleming (10)   111
Monica Hewitt (10)   111
Sarah Kelly (11)   112
Amanda McMillan (10)   113
Khal Cullen (11)   114
Caragh Foreman (11)   115
Cassie McAveety (10)   116
Fiona Gavin (10)   117
Erin Nelson (11)   118

Kayrene Donnelly (11)   119
D'Arcy Robertson (11)   120

St Helen's Primary School, Condorrant
Jordan Pirrie (8)   120
Stephanie Cairney (9)   121
Morgan Dillon (8)   121
Robyn Kerins (9)   121
Mark Beaton (9)   122
Joanne McLaren (9)   122
Shannon McAuley (9)   122

St John the Baptist Primary School, Roscor
Nathan Gallagher (10)   123
Aisling Maguire (10)   123
Aimee McDonnell (11)   123
Michelle Keenan (10)   124
Aimee Freeburn (10)   124
Serena Gallagher (10)   125
Damien Lawn (9)   125
Jenny Campbell (10)   126
Ryan Gormley (11)   126
Cáolan Travers (10)   127
Conor Gormley (9)   127
Philip Denning (10)   128
Catherine Shaw (10)   128

St Mary's Primary School, Maghery
Brendan Haveron (10)   128
Ben Crealey (10)   129
Neil McConville (9)   129
Roisin McConville (10)   130
Lee McConville (9)   130
Emmet McParland (10)   131
Shannon Tennyson (11)   131
Coleen Cushnahan (10)   132
Eoin Tennyson (9)   132
Eimhear Cushnahan (10)   133
Conor Devlin (9)   133
Tiarnan Branagh (9)   134
Paul Devine (10)   134

Orlaith Robinson (10)   135
Iarlaith Hendron (10)   135

St Nicholas' CW Primary School, Cardiff
Lee Thomas (9)   136
Luke Williams (9)   136
Taylor Rees Maher (10)   137
Emily Kathryn Azzopardi (9)   137
Hannah Jane Clarke (9)   138
Lukas Wallis (8)   138
Paige Williams (10)   139
Chloe Newman (8)   139
Emily Ann Thomas (10)   140
Rachel Maria Jones (10)   140
Nathan Stephens (10)   141
Thomas Harvey (9)   141
Chloe Bridgeman (10)   142
Michael Foley (11)   142

Ysgol Cynlais, Swansea
Chantelle Morgan (10)   143
Clarice Critchley (10)   143
Stacey Griffin (10)   144
Siân Poynton (8)   144
Daniel Smith (10)   145
Naiomi Williams (8)   145
Faye Lewis (9)   146
Luc Caines (9)   146
Katie Morgan (9)   147
David Griffiths (9)   147
Kieran Bufton (8)   148
Dee Lewis (7)   148
Daisy Lovering (7)   148
Luke Smith (8)   149
Joshua Taylor (10)   149
Laura Harper (7)   149
Kathryn Potter (10)   150
Megan Robini (10)   151
Ffion Griffiths (10)   151
Elliot Antcliff (10)   152
Finley Topping (8)   153

The Poems

Favourite Colours

My face is bright sparkling red with steam blustering out of my ears
with rage.
Burning hot red fire gets put out by freezing cold water.
Sloppy, slimy red sauce swirling on my freshly made pizza.
Brightly shining, the red pen is very, very famous.
Beautiful smelling red roses blowing in the summer's breeze.
My bright orange pencil always sharp and never running out.
An orange is a healthy organic orange fruit, it is delicious.
Irn-Bru is a fizzy orange, juicy drink, a bit like lemonade.
There are a lot of orange things in pictures.
Bananas are also healthy, organic yellow fruit, they are scrumptious.
The sun is a bright yellow ball of fire and it is very, very hot.
The scissors in our class are yellow at the top, they are weird.
The deep blue sea lies next to the hot, hot beach.
The sky so blue, maybe one day I'll touch it or maybe even you will.
My cousin's dog so colourful, it is because it's black and white.

Nairn Brown

Happiness

Happiness is when I see my nana, a big smile comes like a banana.
Happiness is when I go to the seaside, the golden sand tickles my
toes,

like a feather.
Happiness is like dancing on the beach with soft music

like a soft pillow.
Happiness is the colour baby blue that reminds me of my cousin.
Happiness is eating ice cream on a dazzling hot day.

Ciara Fitzsimmons

Arsenal

A rsenal, the greatest, hot, on fire
R un fast scoring amazing goals
S houting, singing, they've scored a goal!
E normous stadium called The Emirates
N il, the score to Manchester United
A rsene Wenger, the top manager
L Junberg scores like a tornado.

That's Arsenal!

Alvin Mathew Baby

Autumn Signs

Autumn's here at last, it's true
The falling leaves are a clue

All the animals are now asleep
In a sleep that is very deep

The birds go somewhere warm
They fly together in a swarm

At the end of October, Hallowe'en night
People dress up and give you a fright

Berries and nuts, their growth complete
Come and pick, they're quite a treat

This poem is all about autumn
A season which will never be forgotten.

Patrick McNamee (10)
Altayeskey Primary School. Magherafelt

My Cousin

Elise is my sweet cousin,
She is my very best friend,
We call each other nearly every day,
She is really fun and kind,
And a bit like me!
Even though we live far apart,
We still are very close.
I hope to see her very soon,
I really just can't wait!
And when I hear her coming,
I'll be waiting at the gate . . .

Now we're jumping on the trampoline,
She's like a bouncy ball,
A spring escaping from a clock!
You can see her from Fermanagh to Donemana,
That's my cousin Elise.

Amy Grier (11)
Artigarvan Primary School, Artigarvan

My Mum And Dad

My mum and dad are rosy-red,
Just like the summer warmth.
Mum's hugs are like lying in a cosy bed,
She's like the bright light of the moon.
Dad's a thick warm jumper,
Like a funny kids' show,
But one thing's for sure,
They can both be red-hot chilli peppers,
I mean who isn't?
Now I hope you like my parents,
I know I really do!

Lauren Smyth (10)
Artigarvan Primary School, Artigarvan

My Friend

My friend is called Melissa,
She loves cats,
But she hates rats!
She sits beside me in school,
She is very chatty,
We sometimes go to the swimming pool.
We have a lot of fun there,
She is like a dolphin,
We play dares,
We have races,
She always wins,
But I'm starting to get better!
Then we go home,
And the fun is all gone!

Victoria Darragh (11)
Artigarvan Primary School, Artigarvan

My Dad

My dad is always there
And cheers me up
When I'm down.
He makes me laugh
When I look sad.
But when I am bad,
He can get pretty mad.
He's like lightning
Or a roaring bear.
But then he cheers up
And puts on silly faces
Or a big smile.
It makes him look like a clown,
But it always cheers me up.

Kelsey Hume (10)
Artigarvan Primary School, Artigarvan

Dad

Some dads are kind.
Some are fun and interesting.
But mine is not ordinary,
He takes me places,
And his shiny cold head
Makes a shine in the light.

His warm soft hands
Rub my head,
He goes to work at 6.30am,
He comes back at 5.00pm,
He says hello,
He gets his dinner,
Lays his back on the sofa,
Slumps and tosses to get comfy
And watches television.

But he's always
A shooting star
Above everyone!

Samara Britton (10)
Artigarvan Primary School, Artigarvan

My Mum

My mum is bright,
She is the summer breeze,
She is a cosy living room,
She is sunny,
She is a thick cotton jacket,
She is a cosy warm bed,
She is a comedy film,
She is the scalding warm gravy
On my creamy spuds!

Jordan Trevor Cochrane (10)
Artigarvan Primary School, Artigarvan

My Gran

My gran is as warm as the sun,
And as busy as a bee.
She's a better knitter than my granda,
That's for sure!
She never shouts but always laughs,
She would never leave you out,
Oh, not my gran!
She comes to get me every week.
She cooks the best food you could ever eat!
She's the best at Christmas,
Buying you all the presents you would ever need.
At night we jump on the sofa together
And cuddle up to watch some TV.

Chloe Anderson (10)
Artigarvan Primary School, Artigarvan

A Pesty Brother

My pesty brother,
Always tells me what to do,
He never lets me play the PlayStation.
He is as lively as a horse,
Sometimes he is as lazy as a hippo,
And fills the sofa.
He does not like school
Sometimes he is all right!
He likes to farm,
And likes to collect chestnuts,
He plays with them all the time.

Rachel Kee (10)
Artigarvan Primary School, Artigarvan

My Best Friend

My friend is a shy puppy,
She is a tall tree
And like the summer breeze,
She is like a flower in bud
And like the buds of May,
But sometimes,
When she's angry,
She's like a furious rushing sea,
On a stormy night!
But Rachel is still
My best friend,
She is the most special best friend
I could ever have!

Emma Baird (11)
Artigarvan Primary School, Artigarvan

My Uncle Rodger Laird

My uncle is called Rodger,
He can get curious,
He can be very furious.
He can be kind to me,
Sometimes he can be hard to see.
My friends all like him too,
Because of what he can do!
He is a hardworking man,
And he is a Rangers' fan,
And that is Rodger Laird.

Reece Laird (10)
Artigarvan Primary School, Artigarvan

My Dad

My dad is as big as a mountain in our small PlayStation room,
A cloudy man in his work clothes,
A long lamp post,
A summery man,
A cheerful film he is,
The only time he's as mad as a bull is when Manchester United
Cannot score,
He will roar at the television one hundred times,
But after all the excitement, you think he's roaring,
But he's really snoring!

Craig Peters (11)
Artigarvan Primary School, Artigarvan

My Dad

My dad is techno-mad,
He likes to laugh and play,
He's jolly, maybe slightly fat,
But when he's at computers,
He's at it all day!
His eyes are staring like he's deeply in love,
But when I say, 'Come play,'
He'll play with me and stay.
He's like an on-off switch,
He's happy when he's on,
And grumpy when he's off!
I don't know what to call him,
He is a mix up!
That's why I love my dad,
He never goes away,
Until he goes to work,
Then he gets a hug, a kiss,
Then he goes,
While I shout,
'I love you Dad!'

Emma Elliott (10)
Artigarvan Primary School, Artigarvan

My Parrot Twin

My parrot twin
Chirrups and chats all day long,
She is very colourful.
When she is in a bad mood,
She blows up
Like a red volcano.
But when she is in a good mood,
Her wings spread open sometimes.
She clutters her nest,
And chews her food,
And gulps her drink,
And stares about like a hawk,
She flies to the kitchen when dinner is ready
But some seeds are always left.
She is the 'always OK' one
And the best twin in the world
I would be a bulb without a light
Without her!

Alison Baird (11)
Artigarvan Primary School, Artigarvan

My Sister, Mad As Can Be!

My sister is red,
She's the summer warmth.
She's always so active,
But in the morning,
She's not such fun!
When she comes home from school,
She's even worse!
She goes mental when I say
She's on the internet.
But at the end of the day
She's my pillow to lie on!

Zoë Scott (10)
Artigarvan Primary School, Artigarvan

Daddy!

My daddy is very tanned,
He is the summer warmth,
He is the best dad,
He is the best chef,
He likes to be a lazy lump,
But when I get him up off the sofa,
He likes to play a game,
He is really active when he wants to be,
He does everything for me
So I do everything for him!
He is the best daddy
That is Daddy Huey!

Lauren Huey (10)
Artigarvan Primary School, Artigarvan

My Mum

My mum is the best mum in the world,
She bought me a dog,
It tried to eat a frog!
She is like a mouse,
She is sunny,
She is like an emotional film.
She is like the chicken in my soup!

Jack Dinsmore (10)
Artigarvan Primary School, Artigarvan

My Mum

My mum is pink,
She is sunny like warmth,
She sits in the living room,
She is funny at all times,
A happy film,
A thick warming soup!

Billy-Joe Thompson (10)
Artigarvan Primary School, Artigarvan

My Dad

My dad is the motorbike man,
He is the wide open door,
He can be stormy and very angry,
And sometimes very warm,
He is a horror movie ready to strike,
And sometimes tells me to take a hike!
But he is very funny and plays with me,
That is my dad!

Luke Hayes (10)
Artigarvan Primary School, Artigarvan

I Have A Shark In Me

I have a shark in me
Diving deeply
Swimming secretly
Searching quickly
Gobbling proudly
People feel scared
And he feels happy.

Nia Heard (8) & Sam Mogford (9)
Blaenhonddan Primary School, Neath

Puppy

I have a puppy in me
Running madly
Loudly barking
Messing, digging
Playing funnily
People like him
And he thinks he's the best.

Alana Wigley, Alyx Golding (8) & Charlie Arbourne
Blaenhonddan Primary School, Neath

Fireworks

The silver sparkler shines in the dark.
The speeding rocket flies into the black sky.
The rumbling volcano explodes into the air.
The flashing flying saucer speeds to the stars.
The golden rain falls from the sky to the ground.

Owen Thomas, Cameron Harvey & Nathan Jones (7)
Blaenhonddan Primary School, Neath

Hallowe'en Fun!

The ivory skeleton rattles on the rooftop.
The transparent ghost floats into the moonlight.
The magical cat turns the poor prince into a fat frog.
The evil witch makes a poisonous potion in her cauldron.
The flying pumpkin lights up the pitch-black sky.

Ellie Jenks, Aaron Jones & Oliver Harry (7)
Blaenhonddan Primary School, Neath

Noisy Fireworks

A whizzing rocket flew to the stars.
The shiny golden rain fell from the sky.
A flying saucer whizzed to the moon.
The coloured Catherine wheel spun in the dark.
A noisy volcano erupted into the darkness.

Matthew James, Thomas Hames & Sam Owen (7)
Blaenhonddan Primary School, Neath

Fireworks!

A whizzing Catherine wheel spins in the silver moonlight.
A flashing sparkler glitters in the darkness.
A bursting rocket explodes into the air.
A sparkling golden rain pours into the sky.
A zooming flying saucer soars into space.

Georgia Parsons, Eve Hanford & Gabrielle Lewis (7)
Blaenhonddan Primary School, Neath

Fireworks Light The Night!

The shiny rocket shot into the sky.
The big flying saucer spun around my head.
The hot volcano burst into showers of rain.
The shiny Catherine wheel swirled around the stick.
The sparkling golden rain exploded in the garden.

Steffan Parry-Howells, Alex Morris (7) & Liam Evans (8)
Blaenhonddan Primary School, Neath

Bonfire Night

The shimmering sparkler sparkles in the darkness.
The loud Big Ben booms in the dark sky.
The showering golden rain scatters in the starlight.
The colourful Catherine wheel spins in the moonlight.
The squealing rocket wiggles into the air.

Elin James, Lara Berni (7) & Olivia Michael (8)
Blaenhonddan Primary School, Neath

A Poem For Hallowe'en

The black bats fly in the moonlight.
The fat pumpkin lights up the street.
The hollow ghost shouts, *'Boo!'* in the woods.
The bony skeleton dances in the house.
The wicked witch rides on her magic broomstick.
The creepy cat sneaks into the haunted house.

Oban Crossman, Connell Doherty & Ben Heywood (7)
Blaenhonddan Primary School, Neath

I Have An Owl In Me

I have an owl in me
Sleeping quietly
Silently flying
Noisily hooting
Gulping greedily
People think they're harmless
They are very intelligent.

Joe Humphries (8) & Ryan Clarkson (9)
Blaenhonddan Primary School, Neath

I Have A Monkey In Me

I have a monkey in me
Eating bananas luckily
Slowly climbing trees.
Roughly throwing bananas
The people are amazed
The monkey feels proud.

Jessica Rosser (8)
Blaenhonddan Primary School, Neath

I Have A Puppy In Me

I have a puppy in me
Sprinting happily
Quietly sleeping
Loudly barking
Whining sadly
People are amazed
He is proud!

Joshua Rhys Thomas & Ieuan David Stradling (9)
Blaenhonddan Primary School, Neath

I Have A Butterfly In Me

I have a butterfly in me,
Fluttering elegantly,
Flying quickly,
Landing quietly,
Proudly landing,
People are mystified,
And the butterflies feel scared.

Amy Davies & Caroline Millan (8)
Blaenhonddan Primary School, Neath

I Have A Kangaroo In Me

I have a kangaroo in me
Exploring excitingly
Happily hopping
Quietly bouncing
Adventuring sluggishly
People are scared
But he feels very calm.

Joseph Cornwall (8) & Katherine Thompson
Blaenhonddan Primary School, Neath

The Cool Killer Shark

I have a shark in me.
Hunting slyly.
Slowly watching.
Quickly swimming.
Killing fiercely.
People are super-terrified
And the shark feels fabulous.

Aaron James Harvey (8)
Blaenhonddan Primary School, Neath

Haiku

Crunchy leaves falling
Walking in the autumn breeze
It is harvest time.

Lewis Mainwaring (8)
Blaenhonddan Primary School, Neath

I Have A Monkey In Me

I have a monkey in me
Strangely reacting
Quietly eating
Running quickly
Swinging crazily
People are laughing
And he thinks he's
        clever!

Caitlin Morgan (8)
Blaenhonddan Primary School, Neath

I Have A Snake In Me

Slithering slyly.
Slowly creeping.
Silently waiting.
Snapping loudly.
People are tortured by it.
The snake is satisfied.

Ellie Lewis & Sam Freeman (8)
Blaenhonddan Primary School, Neath

Autumn - Haiku

Hedgehogs are crawling,
Squirrels are eating chestnuts,
In the autumn wind.

Caroline Millan & Amy Davies (8)
Blaenhonddan Primary School, Neath

I Have A Bluebird In Me.

I have a bluebird in me.
Flying happily.
Proudly singing.
Quietly sitting.
Sleeping gracefully.
People think it's funny
But the bluebird is scared.

Zoe Dowling (8)
Blaenhonddan Primary School, Neath

A Hallowe'en Spell

(Or How To Get Rid Of Your Teachers)

Bats and rats
And witches' hats.
Snakes and frogs
And howling dogs.
Spiders' webs
And hairy legs.
Abracadabra!
Fill this classroom full of bones
And turn the teachers into stones!

Cameron Dobbs, Liam Griffiths (7), Liam Goodall, Justin Hearn (8), Jessica Moule, Niome Andrews, Rebecca Ellis, Mathew Watkins & Liam Miles (10)
Blaenhonddan Primary School, Neath

The Jungle

(Inspired by 'The Door' by Miroslav Holub)

Walk into the jungle
Maybe there's a lion roaring like thunder
Or a monkey swinging in the trees.
Walk into the jungle
Maybe you'll hear the rustle in the trees
Or a cheetah dashing through the wind
Or a snake rattling through the bushes.
Walk into the jungle
Even if there's a snake slithering around you
Even if there's a dead tiger on the ground
Even if you're tangled in cobwebs.
Walk into the jungle
At least you're safe and sound.

Benjamin Powell (9)
Blaenhonddan Primary School, Neath

The Changing Seasons

Autumn, the leaves crunching.
The breeze blows through my hair.
Summer, the golden sun shining brightly through the open window.
Winter, cold white snow covers the grass like a blanket.
Spring, flowers sprouting and opening.
I watch through the window.

Ffion Williams (9)
Blaenhonddan Primary School, Neath

The Castle

(Inspired by 'The Door' by Miroslav Holub)

Walk into the castle
Maybe there's a scary ghost
A man called Frankenstein
Or a spider's web.
Walk into the castle
Maybe you'll hear bats flying
Or a ghost going *'Ooooo!'*
Or a creaking door slamming.
Walk into the castle
Even if there's a scary monster
Even if there's a bat flying
Even if you see a big scary monster
Walk into the castle.
At least we'll have fun.

Rhys Chapman (8)
Blaenhonddan Primary School, Neath

I'm Staying In The Villa After Swimming Today

I'm staying in the villa after swimming today.
I'd rather stay in bed
Pretending that I haven't been fed.
I'll say I'm very hungry
And she'll give me something to eat.
I'll show her my belly and pull it in so tight
And she'll give me a treat.

Bethan Mulligan (9)
Blaenhonddan Primary School, Neath

Swimming Is The Worst Sport

Swimming is the worst sport
I cannot stay afloat!
Jumping doesn't help
Water makes me yelp.

I dread going in the water
When my friend jumps in, his legs go like a motor!
I dream of chocolate in my head
I'd rather be eating it instead.

There is no swimming anymore
I like to be on the floor!
My legs are not built for the sea
But that's just me!

Louis Evans (9)
Blaenhonddan Primary School, Neath

I Have A Little Brother

I have a little brother,
He dreams of many things
He dreams of being big and strong,
And eating lots of things.

He dreams of being famous
He dreams of being cool
He dreams of playing tennis
In his swimming pool.

He dreams of having powers,
And life on Mars.
Meeting lots of aliens
And having a laugh,

I think it's a bunch of nonsense
But maybe he's right,
But if this is true
I will have a jolly good fright.

Rhys Austin (9)
Blaenhonddan Primary School, Neath

I'm Staying Home From Nan's Today

I'm staying home from Nan's today.
I'll say I've got a bad bone.
I'll toss and turn and grumble and groan!
I'll claim I have stomach ache.
I'll say I'm sore.
I'll fake I'm dizzy and fall on the floor.

Nia Parry-Howells (10)
Blaenhonddan Primary School, Neath

My Favourite Sport

Football is my favourite sport
I play it all the time.

Football is the greatest.
I love watching, it playing it
And winning it.

I run down the line with the football
I cross the ball in and then it's a goal!
When I score I do a mad celebration.

It is so much fun
Playing football in the sun.

Dylan Matthews (9)
Blaenhonddan Primary School, Neath

Autumn

It's the time of autumn
When the leaves are turning brown
They fall off the trees
I love the autumn breeze.

My hair tousled in the air
The robins hopping without dropping
Bees stinging,
It's the last of summer.

Ellie Plumb-Darrell (9)
Blaenhonddan Primary School, Neath

Oviraptor Gets Everything

Oviraptor gets everything
He gets bikes, he gets money
He also gets that baby's dummy!
And every day of the week
He gets silly hats that make him look funny.
When Oviraptor walks up to you
He stares, he cries
And then he gets his claws on you!

Connor Jones (9)
Blaenhonddan Primary School, Neath

My Dog Ate My Pencil

My dog ate my pencil.
The greedy pup.
He went in my schoolbag
And swallowed it up.
My dog ate my pencil.
I hope he will be OK.
I need to take him
To the vet today.
My dog ate my pencil.
He gobbled it all.
I shouldn't have taken him
To school at all.

Natalie Jones (9)
Blaenhonddan Primary School, Neath

Seasons

In winter, I pick up the icy snow in my cold winter hands.
In summer the warm hot sun shines so bright across the world
like a blanket.
In autumn the crusty brown leaves fall off the tall, old, oak tree.
In spring the sweet new heads of the flowers start popping up
in the warm sunny day.

Eleanor Collins (10)
Blaehonddan Primary School, Neath

Seasons

In autumn the crunchy leaves fall to the ground.
In summer the hot sun shines upon the grassy green hills.
In winter the white fluffy snow falls and covers the green grass.
In spring the flowers pop up and brighten the world.

Robyn Tucker (9)
Blaenhonddan Primary School, Neath

What Does My Dog Dream Of?

What does my dog dream of?
He dreams of getting lucky
And having a spotty puppy.
Dreams of long walks
And he dreams he can talk.

My dog dreamed of being loved
And that wish came true.
Now he has a family to love
And to live with too.

Tamara Jones (9)
Blaenhonddan Primary School, Neath

I'll Be Too Late

I'm not going to rugby today
I'll just catch a cold.
And when I get my top on
I'll be too late.

I'm not going to swimming today
I'll just get all wet.
And when I jump in
I will just sink.

I'm not going to Cubs today
I'll just get all hot.
And when I go
My friends will not show up.

Robert Curtis (9)
Blaenhonddan Primary School, Neath

Anger

Anger is red like a blazing fire,
It sounds like a firework in the sky,
It tastes like a fireball sizzling in my mouth,
It smells like smoke rising from the hillside,
It looks like a monster invading the world,
It feels like the bark of a tree in my hand,
It reminds me of hate.

Charlotte Thomas (9)
Brynmenyn Primary School, Bridgend

Happiness

The colour of happiness is bright yellow.
The taste of happiness is like ripe yellow bananas.
The smell of happiness is like beautiful candyfloss.
Happiness looks like a big bunch of flowers.
Happiness sounds like two joyful birds.

Elle Edwards (7)
Brynmenyn Primary School, Bridgend

Anger

Anger is the colour of grey and black.
Anger smells like the puffing smoke steaming from my head.
Anger tastes like insects crawling into my mouth.
Anger looks like my skeleton about to pop out.
Anger sounds like my ear shaking like mad.
Anger feels like somebody punching and kicking me and will not stop.

Daniel Elward (8)
Brynmenyn Primary School, Bridgend

Anger

Anger is a red dashing devil.
It sounds like an evil laugh.
It tastes like a fireball whizzing around your mouth.
It smells like a chilli frying on the ground.
It looks like zooming on petrol.
It feels like fire burning my skin.
Anger reminds me of the Devil.

Shane Hill (9)
Brynmenyn Primary School, Bridgend

Silence

Silence is a storm of snowflakes.
It sounds like a wind blowing towards me.
It tastes like plain water going down my throat.
It smells like daffodils everywhere around me.
It looks like fishes glittering in the sea.
It feels like something small moving in my hand.
Silence reminds of reading a book in silence.

Floyd Panizales (8)
Brynmenyn Primary School, Bridgend

Happiness

Happiness is like a yellow flower in the summer.
It sounds like a bird playing a tune.
It tastes like a chocolate cake with cream.
It smells like a rose on a summer's day.
It looks like a bee buzzing happily.
It feels like velvet on a dress.
Happiness reminds me of two rabbits hopping in spring.

Lucy Morgan (8)
Brynmenyn Primary School, Bridgend

Fear

Fear is dark red and grey.
Fear tastes like a cheesy sock.
Fear smells like a dirty dustbin.
Fear looks like a lonely smelly street.
Fear sounds like a skunk farting.
Fear feels like a slimy goldfish.

Bethan Thomas (7)
Brynmenyn Primary School, Bridgend

Love

Love is bright red like a strawberry.
Love is peaceful like having a sleep.
Love smells like cherries.
Love looks like a big heart.
Love sounds like joyful songs.
Love feels smooth.

Cohan Lewis (9)
Brynmenyn Primary School, Bridgend

What's Life?

Life is like a book of poems.
Life is like a rainbow of colours.
Life is sometimes unfair and sad.
Life is something that will never end.
Life is full of fun and games.
Life is something money can't buy.
Life is like the big blue sky.
Life is things we don't want to do.
Life is better than rubies and diamonds.
Life is dangerous when we don't know what's there.
Life is when we stop and stare.
Life is like a ghost that is our shadow.
Life is like a gift from God.
Life is like a shimmering stream.
Life is something we all love.
Life is light, as light as a dove.
Life is something that everyone needs.
Life is full of laughter and good deeds.
Life isn't perfect, we all have our moments.
Life is something we shouldn't waste.
Life is something we can all taste.
Life is something we all love.
Life!

Katie Ellis (9)
Brynmenyn Primary School, Bridgend

Love

Love is pink like my wordless strong heart
It sounds like a calm gentle breeze
It tastes like fluffy pink candyfloss
It smells like a strawberry lollipop fresh from the stall
It looks like a pink fuzzy slipper, so comfy
It feels like a soft purple bobble hat
Love reminds me of a bright red rose.

Loren Bennett (8)
Brynmenyn Primary School, Bridgend

Feelings

Happiness
Happiness is golden like the beaming hot sun.
It sounds like singing birds sitting on a bendy branch.
It tastes like chocolate cake in the night.
It smells like blossom flying in the fresh air.
It looks like the sunset looking down on us.
It feels like soft fluffy candyfloss.
Happiness reminds me of my mum's cuddles before school.

Fear
Fear is orange like a big orange fire.
It sounds like screaming voices all around me.
It tastes like vinegar on a piece of apple pie.
It smells like smoke flying above me.
It looks like a pack of wolves, just so hungry.
It feels like you have burnt your finger.
Fear reminds me of a little girl dying from hunger.

Nia Gronow (9)
Brynmenyn Primary School, Bridgend

Fear

Fear is black like your body is screaming at you.
It sounds like a roaring tiger coming towards you.
It tastes like the blood leaving and then coming back into your body.
It smells like a rotten egg on your face, then going down
                                    to your shivering feet.
It looks like a horrible monster is coming towards you.
It feels like stinging nettles on your face.
Fear reminds me of being nasty!

Keiran Herbert (9)
Brynmenyn Primary School, Bridgend

Happiness

Happiness is black like a big gust of wind.
It sounds like people laughing and playing.
It tastes like fresh sweets.
It smells like a scented flower.
It looks like a sunny sunset.
It feels like a warm loving hug.
Happiness reminds me of the summer holiday.

Daisy Faulkner (8)
Brynmenyn Primary School, Bridgend

Autumn

Turning cold,
Birds that sing,
Pine cones and conkers,
Green, brown, orange and red,
Crunchy leaves,
Trick or treat and fireworks,
That's why autumn is special to me.

Lily Ile (7)
Brynmenyn Primary School, Bridgend

Autumn

Autumn days when the flowers are blooming
and the leaves are falling,
the birds will be singing their songs
and you'll hear everyone sing along.

Grace Ellis (7)
Brynmenyn Primary School, Bridgend

Happiness

Happiness is yellow like a yummy banana in a fruit bowl.
It sounds like kids running around and singing loudly.
It tastes like a chocolate egg on Easter Day.
It smells like a flower in a lovely garden.
It looks like chocolate and strawberry sauce going on ice cream.
It feels like soft hair blowing in the wind.
Happiness reminds me of rabbits bouncing around everywhere.

Shauna Griffiths (9)
Brynmenyn Primary School, Bridgend

Fear

Fear is black like a vulture waiting for its prey.
It sounds like wild jackals running around.
It tastes like cold gravy on a gloomy night.
It smells like a cesspit overflowing.
It looks like an angry bull in an arena.
It feels like the wind pushing me to the wrong path

It reminds me of . . . *evil!*

Ben Page (9)
Brynmenyn Primary School, Bridgend

Happiness

Happiness is a bright·yellow colour like the sun.
Happiness feels like candyfloss.
Happiness smells like fresh cut grass.
Happiness looks like a bunch of grapes.

Brook Lewis (7)
Brynmenyn Primary School, Bridgend

Feelings

Love
Love is like a pink heart floating in the sky.
Love sounds like a pretty bird singing in the morning.
Love tastes like a strawberry dipped in melted chocolate.
Love smells like popcorn fresh from the stall.
Love looks like a soft little kitten.
Love reminds me of my dog Bonnie.

Happiness
Happiness is like true friends forever.
Happiness sounds like a choir singing at Christmas.
Happiness tastes like a chocolate cake.
Happiness smells like chocolate chip cookies.
Happiness looks like a person with a smile on their face.
Happiness feels like doing sums in maths.
Happiness reminds me of my best friend Natalie.

Rachel Randall (8)
Brynmenyn Primary School, Bridgend

Anger

Anger is purple like a raging violet.
It sounds like a World War II bomb hitting me inside.
It tastes like sour vinegar.
It smells like a bombed prison cell.
It looks like a raging monster.
It feels like a storm of lightning.
Anger reminds me of torture!

Joseph Williams (9)
Brynmenyn Primary School, Bridgend

Happiness

Happiness is yellow like a swaying daffodil.
It sounds like a crowd laughing in the distance.
It tastes like my favourite food sprinkled with lots of salt.
It smells like a fresh pure scent.
It looks like my favourite sight, it's so nice.
It feels so smooth.
Happiness reminds me of fun.

Adam Cooke (9)
Brynmenyn Primary School, Bridgend

Autumn

The trees are becoming bare
the leaves are on the ground
as I walk they make
a crispy and crunchy sound.

The nights are growing darker
there's fear in the air
Hallowe'en is near
everyone beware!

Red and gold is everywhere
even in the sky
the smell in the air is smoky
as the bonfires glow and fireworks fly

Jack Frost makes a visit
as autumn moves along
the mornings are getting colder
time to wrap up warm.

Bradley Newman (7)
Brynmenyn Primary School, Bridgend

Happiness Is . . .

Happiness is when I'm playing 'catch' with my friends.
Happiness is when I'm eating bubblegum flavour ice cream,
                                      on a hot sunny day.
Happiness is going for a bicycle ride with my mum.
Happiness is eating a Sunday roast dinner with all my family.
Happiness is when I get gifts for my birthday.
Happiness is when I give gifts to my friends for their birthdays.
Happiness is when we make Rice Krispie buns.

Megan Reid (8)
Cookstown Primary School, Cookstown

Autumn

Autumn is finally here
Squirrels are hunting for nuts
Days are getting darker earlier
It's time for bonfires and fireworks
To light up high in the sky.
Hedgehogs are making a bed of leaves
Moving around slowly
Birds migrate to warmer countries
Leaves are gently falling like butterflies
On Hallowe'en night, children go trick or treating
Around houses for sweets.
I really, really like autumn.

Jamie Lindsay (10)
Cookstown Primary School, Cookstown

Happiness Is . . .

Happiness is when I share with my friends.
Happiness is when I go to church to learn about God and Jesus.
Happiness is when I go to school to learn more sums.
Happiness is when I help my mummy to do the housework.
Happiness is when I make new friends at school.

Jessica Stewart (8)
Cookstown Primary School, Cookstown

Happiness Is . . .

Happiness is drinking hot chocolate.
Happiness is listening to the birds sing.
Happiness is eating 'Ready Salted Pringles'.
Happiness is going on holiday to Newcastle.
Happiness is getting off school for Hallowe'en.
Happiness is eating a bar of Galaxy.
Happiness is helping my daddy deliver Shaws sweets.
Happiness is going home and watching a film because
                         there is no school on Saturday.
Happiness is when I am playing football.
Happiness is going to a party and dressing up!

Joshua Glendinning (7)
Cookstown Primary School, Cookstown

Happiness Is . . .

Happiness is singing in the junior choir.
Happiness is early morning, getting up and dressing up
in my school uniform and then going to school.
Happiness is when I meet Mr Downing.
Happiness is when I wake up with Ryan and Jill.

Megan McCrea (7)
Cookstown Primary School, Cookstown

Happiness Is . . .

Happiness is hearing the junior choir sing.
Happiness is at the swimming pool with my friend.
Happiness is at Hallowe'en because I can trick or treat
                         with my cousins Beth and Rose.
Happiness is meeting Mr Downing.
Happiness is Brownies!

Tia Warnock (7)
Cookstown Primary School, Cookstown

Happiness Is . . .

Happiness is going to the beach with my family.
Happiness is eating a big Galaxy bar on a Friday night.
Happiness is dipping a marshmallow in a chocolate fountain.
Happiness is going to 'Buddies' after school club.
Happiness is going to Hallowe'en parties with my friends.
Happiness is opening presents at Christmas.
Happiness is going to school and seeing my new principal,
                                                    Mr Downing.
Happiness is playing in the playground with my friends.
Happiness is meeting my friends Matthew, Ryan, Adam M,
                                            Luke and Steven.
Happiness is going to the Leisure Centre.
Happiness is going to the pool.
Happiness is doing PE outside every Friday.

Danny Kerr (7)
Cookstown Primary School, Cookstown

Happiness Is . . .

Happiness is going to the pool on Friday,
Happiness is staying up late,
Happiness is watching the sun shine in the morning,
Happiness is planting a flower and watching it grow,
Happiness is having a harvest service,
Happiness is having Hallowe'en and Christmas,
Happiness is holding a snake on holiday,
Happiness is fishing with my dad,
Happiness is helping animals survive the winter!

Curtis Hodgett (8)
Cookstown Primary School, Cookstown

Happiness Is . . .

Happiness is sharing my dolls with my sisters Robyn and Alex.
Happiness is being in the Junior Choir.
Happiness is going to church to learn more about Jesus and God.
Happiness is going to school to learn more sums.
Happiness is dressing up and then going trick or treating
                                        with my sisters.
Happiness is going to the Argory with my class.
Happiness is going to the swimming pool with my family.
Happiness is playing with my pets.
Happiness is going out for a meal with my family to the Royal.
Happiness is playing with my friends Grace, Sarah, Claudia,
                                        Lauren, Lois and Ellie.
Happiness is helping my daddy to feed my cat Lucky.

Lois Cooke (8)
Cookstown Primary School, Cookstown

Happiness Is . . .

Happiness is sharing my toys with my friends Lois, Megan,
                                        Jessica and Shannon.
Happiness is singing in the Junior School.
Happiness is moving into my new house and getting my own room!
Happiness is going to the Argory to find out about Tommy
And going to Parkanaur to find out about the weather.
Happiness is riding my pony called Jimmy Joe.
Happiness is playing with my rabbit called Thumper.
Happiness is getting my hair curled for my daddy's birthday.

Claudia Wylie (7)
Cookstown Primary School, Cookstown

Happiness Is . . .

Happiness is playing with my two brothers and sisters.
Happiness is going to school and doing my work.
Happiness is when it is my birthday party.
Happiness is when it is soon Xmas when I get lots and lots
of presents.
Happiness is when it is Hallowe'en because I get to trick or treat
with my sisters and my brothers.
Happiness is when I meet Mr Downing.
Happiness is when I get to play with my friends.
Happiness is when we go on trips from school.
Happiness is when I go to the beach with my family.

Shantel Shannon (7)
Cookstown Primary School, Cookstown

Happiness Is . . .

Happiness is to see the flowers bloom.
Happiness is to hear nature coming out soon.
Happiness is to ride my bicycle with my mum.
Happiness is to see birds hopping on the grass.
Happiness is to see all my friends in the entire school.
Happiness is to go and meet new friends.
Happiness is to learn about Tommy Bond.

Olivia Woods (7)
Cookstown Primary School, Cookstown

Happiness Is . . .

Happiness is building pig feeders on the farm.
Happiness is playing with my dogs Flipper and Dipper.
Happiness is wrestling my twelve-year-old cousin.
Happiness is staying in bed on Saturday.

Matthew Crooks (7)
Cookstown Primary School, Cookstown

Happiness Is . . .

Happiness is sitting down in the living room watching TV
                                        on Friday night.
Happiness is eating a big bar of Galaxy.
Happiness is eating a big Sunday dinner.
Happiness is going to Magherafelt to see my granny.
Happiness is going to the swimming pool with my family.
Happiness is at home playing with my friends.
Happiness is playing at Hallowe'en with my friend Lee.
Happiness is eating a big KFC on a Sunday.
Happiness is playing football with my friends.

Steven Arrell (8)
Cookstown Primary School, Cookstown

Happiness Is . . .

Happiness is going to the swimming pool.
Happiness is playing with my friends.
Happiness is watching TV.
Happiness is going to the after school club.
Happiness is meeting our new principal Mr Downing.
Happiness is sharing with my friends.
Happiness is going to school.

Nathen Espie (7)
Cookstown Primary School, Cookstown

Happiness Is . . .

Happiness is watching TV.
Happiness is when I play with my cousins.
Happiness is when I beat my daddy at TT Super Bikes.
Happiness is going to the Chuck Wagon.
Happiness is going to Ballymena to see my granny.
Happiness is going to the cinema and crunching popcorn!

Daniel Stewart (8)
Cookstown Primary School, Cookstown

Happiness Is . . .

Happiness is having my birthday six days before Christmas.
Happiness is going for a swim in the leisure centre.
Happiness is watching the sunset go down on a Friday evening.
Happiness is decorating the house for Hallowe'en.
Happiness is when I met Mr Downing, our new principal.
Happiness is sitting next to my friend Amy at school.
Happiness is when I met Miss McCormick.
Happiness is when I went to the Argory.
Happiness is when I sit in front of the television to watch
'Midsomer Murders'.
Happiness is playing with my friends in the playground.
Happiness is playing with my Bratz dolls in the sunroom
with my sister Alexandra.

Hannah Mowbray (7)
Cookstown Primary School, Cookstown

Happiness Is . . .

Happiness is going to Buddies' Hallowe'en party.
Happiness is watching a movie with my family.
Happiness is completing my 1500m swimming badge.
Happiness is making Rice Krispie buns with my mummy.
Happiness is finally getting to meet my Uncle Dennis
at Christmas time.
Happiness is playing with my robot on Christmas night.
Happiness is going to the zoo with the Beavers.
Happiness is going on holiday every year.
Happiness is going to the park with my family.

Thomas Simpson (7)
Cookstown Primary School, Cookstown

Happiness Is . . .

Happiness is hot chocolate fudge cake with a strawberry on top
at Hanover House.
Happiness is sharing toys with my friend, Matthew Y.
Happiness is Hallowe'en with beautiful fireworks.
Happiness is going on holiday to Cornwall and playing on the beach
And having a cool drink of lemonade and a barbecue.
Happiness is putting up my decorations on my Christmas tree.
Happiness is going to the swimming pool.
Happiness is going to Buddies After School Club.
Happiness is going to school.
Happiness is going on my bicycle.
Happiness is one night in Cornwall when we went to a party
And we got a drink of Coke and some popcorn.
Happiness is going on a trip with my school.
Happiness is eating an apple.
Happiness is playing in the playground.
Happiness is playing with my kittens at home.

Joel Loughrin (8)
Cookstown Primary School, Cookstown

Happiness Is . . .

Happiness is going pony trekking and finding a lovely horse
called Patch.
Happiness is listening to my sister play the keyboard.
Happiness is going to Brownies in September.
Happiness is reading poetry books and writing poems.
Happiness is having good friends.
Happiness is being in Mrs Miller's class.
Happiness is having lots of fish in my fish tank.
Happiness is having a sister that loves me.

Amy Carson (8)
Cookstown Primary School, Cookstown

Happiness Is . . .

Happiness is going to school to play with my friends and go to PE.
Happiness is going home to do my homework after a long day
                                                    at school.
Happiness is meeting our new principal Mr Downing.
Happiness is going to school to play football.
Happiness is going to school to eat my break and my dinner.
Happiness is going to my dad's house to play with his dog.
Happiness is playing basketball with my baby brother Jordan.

Matthew Young (7)
Cookstown Primary School, Cookstown

Happiness Is . . .

Happiness is when I walk my dog in the forest.
Happiness is when I watch my dog jumping over a big fence,
And it knocks me over and I fall on the grass!
Happiness is watching Man United score a goal.
Happiness is when I do a flip-over on the trampoline.
Happiness is when I see my friend up the town.
Happiness is when I race my daddy on my quad.
Happiness is when I have a football match with my dad.
Happiness is when Mum reads stories to me.

Ryan Wilkinson (8)
Cookstown Primary School, Cookstown

Happiness Is . . .

Happiness is when my granny's cat licks me in the morning.
Happiness is going to band practice and smashing all
                                        the cymbals together.
Happiness is going to Cookstown Youth and scoring lots of goals.
Happiness is going to assembly and listening to Mr Downing.
Happiness is watching Man United playing really well.
Happiness is going to the motorbikes with my daddy.

Jack Dingley (8)
Cookstown Primary School, Cookstown

Happiness Is . . .

Happiness is when I play football.
Happiness is when I go to Adventure World.
Happiness is watching the bands.
Happiness is watching ice-skating.
Happiness is playing with my new cars.
Happiness is playing with my PlayStation.
Happiness is when I watch the football.
Happiness is when I get taught.
Happiness is driving my quad.
Happiness is having my break.

Sam Ferguson (7)
Cookstown Primary School, Cookstown

Happiness Is . . .

Happiness is playing with my guitar in my base in the attic.
Happiness is playing basketball and throwing it through the hoop.
Happiness is going to a disco and dancing.
Happiness is when I held an owl with my best friend Callum.
Happiness is when I stay up late.
Happiness is when I am catching girls.
Happiness is when I am with my mad dad.

Matthew Ruck (7)
Cookstown Primary School, Cookstown

Happiness Is . . .

Happiness is when I ride my bike.
Happiness is when I pat my dog.
Happiness is when I take my dog for a walk.
Happiness is when I go ice skating
Happiness is when I go out to my granny's
Happiness is when I love my granny.
Happiness is when I play football outside.

Andrea Boyle (8)
Cookstown Primary School, Cookstown

Happiness Is . . .

Happiness is when my Auntie Sharon comes for dinner
on Thursday night.
Happiness is singing in the choir on Monday afternoon in school.
Happiness is playing tennis on the beach on Saturday.
Happiness is going shopping for food and at the end I get a treat
for being good.
Happiness is going out with my family for a meal on Saturday night.
Happiness is having a barbecue on Friday night; my favourite is
burgers and sausages.
Happiness is when I race on my yellow go-kart with my cousin Craig
and I win!
Happiness is when I race my dad at running and I beat him.
Happiness is when I go to the park with my mum after school on
Wednesdays.
Happiness is me and my dad playing football and I score six goals
and Dad scores four and I beat him!

Grace Gilmore (7)
Cookstown Primary School, Cookstown

Happiness Is . . .

Happiness is when I meet new friends.
Happiness is when I go to school to learn new things.
Happiness is when I'm enjoying a warm summer's day playing
                                                with my friends.
Happiness is opening presents on Christmas morning
                                        after Santa's been.
Happiness is being with my family.
Happiness is building snowmen on a cold winter's day,
Then cuddling up on the sofa, all cosy and warm, in front of the TV.
Happiness is petting our wee kitten.

Bethany Stoker (7)
Cookstown Primary School, Cookstown

Happiness Is . . .

Happiness is racing my auntie and my daddy on the beach.
Happiness is shooting Sam P with my laser gun in Laserland.
Happiness is playing the Nintendo DS Lite in the hotel.
Happiness is drinking tomato juice in Blue Bar.
Happiness is playing snooker at Skerries.
Happiness is trying a mouthful of Guinness at the seaside.
Happiness is tackling Josh and Scott when playing football
in the playground.
Happiness is playing hide-and-seek at Adventure World.
Happiness is meeting a new friend at the seaside.
Happiness is sunbathing at the beach.
Happiness is my cousin being noisy at 9 o'clock.
Happiness is going to school to learn more things.
Happiness is watching Cars and eating popcorn at the cinema.
Happiness is playing with my naughty cousin at home.
Happiness is playing with my big bicycle out in the garden.
Happiness is watching aeroplanes, eating Jammie Dodgers
And sitting on top of the car at Dublin Airport.

Vincent Wong (7)
Cookstown Primary School, Cookstown

Happiness Is . . .

Happiness is a feeling I get when I play football and score in the net.
Running and dribbling that ball in the park, I could play well
after dark.
Riding my bike, eating sweets,
Visiting my grandparents, they always give me treats.
Smiling faces, nice friendly words,
Visiting places I've never heard.
I have so much fun every day, laughing and smiling,
That I can say *'Happiness is . . .!'*

Jordan Scott (7)
Cookstown Primary School, Cookstown

Happiness Is . . .

Happiness is when my nanny teaches me piano lessons.
Happiness is going on my pink bike and doing wheelies.
Happiness is going to the beach on Sundays.
Happiness is going on holiday to Scotland.
Happiness is going ice-skating at the leisure centre.
Happiness is playing with Chloe, Bethany, Shalanda and Shantel
in the playground.
Happiness is when I play with my boyfriend.
Happiness is when I go to my nanny's.
Happiness is going after Marc and Ryan.
Happiness is when I go for a walk.
Happiness is when I go to the cinema.
Happiness is going on a school trip to Argory.

Chloe Brownlow (7)
Cookstown Primary School, Cookstown

Happiness Is . . .

Happiness is on the bumper cars at Barry's.
Happiness is lying in bed reading a Jacqueline Wilson book.
Happiness is licking a whipped ice cream and sunbathing
at the seaside.
Happiness is zooming around the house on my go-kart.
Happiness is at Christmas time opening all my lovely presents
from Santa.
Happiness is going up to the leisure centre and going to the shop
for a Slush Puppie - I have the blue flavour.
Happiness is when I go to my granny's and granda's house in
Portadown to have dinner and dessert - apple crumble!
Happiness is playing and talking to my best friend Lauren outside.
Happiness is having art with Mrs Wallace
making clay leaves on a Tuesday afternoon.
Happiness is when it is 3 o'clock on the 30th June!

Emily Slaine (8)
Cookstown Primary School, Cookstown

Happiness Is . . .

Happiness is when I go to piano lessons.
Happiness is when I get to see my three horses in the garden.
Happiness is when I am tucked up in bed reading a book.
Happiness is going outside and playing with my friends
on my trampoline.
Happiness is in the car going to the seaside, in the car
I play with my cards.
Happiness is eating dinner with my granda, we have steak,
potatoes, chicken and gravy.
Happiness is when I have chocolate cake at my birthday party.
Happiness is when I go to Portrush and play in the park.
Happiness is going shopping with my mummy and I get lots
of clothes.
Happiness is going to the cinema with my daddy and watching
'Ratatouille' and I eat sweets.
Happiness was when I went to Belfast Zoo and I saw lots and lots
of animals.

Ellie May Parke (7)
Cookstown Primary School, Cookstown

Happiness Is . . .

Happiness is going to violin lessons
Happiness is when I sing the harvest songs at school and do
                                    the actions as well
Happiness is when I pick flowers in the garden
Happiness is when my best friend Emily sleeps over at my house
Happiness is on my quad and I go really fast
Happiness is when I go to my granny's house and draw
Happiness is when I go to school and learn lots of things
Happiness is when I stay up late on a Friday and Saturday night
Happiness is when I go to the cinema and eat sweets.

Lauren Henry (8)
Cookstown Primary School, Cookstown

Happiness Is . . .

Happiness is when I go to piano lessons on a Wednesday.
Happiness is when I go shopping for toys with my mum.
Happiness is when my friends come to play.
Happiness is when I go to football with my dad on Boxing Day.
Happiness is when I go to school to learn more every day.
Happiness is when I go on holiday and splash in the waves
at the beach.
Happiness is when I got my certificate presented in assembly
this morning.
Happiness is when I go to the park with my mum.
Happiness is when I go to my granny's and granda's
to play Monopoly.

Sarah Dorothea Wilson (7)
Cookstown Primary School, Cookstown

Happiness Is . . .

Happiness is playing the piano in my bedroom.
Happiness is when I am tucked up in bed reading Lizzie Zipmouth
by Jacqueline Wilson.
Happiness is zooming round the field on my quad making tracks.
Happiness is walking my dog at home.
Happiness is when I see my granny on Saturday.
Happiness is when Mummy takes me to the swimming pool.
Happiness is when I go to the caravan to play with Erin.
Happiness is eating chocolate cake at Granny's house.
Happiness is baking down at Granny's house.
Happiness is when I go to Brownies.

Grace Miller (8)
Cookstown Primary School, Cookstown

Happiness Is . . .

Happiness is when I go to ballet in my pink tutu and ballet shoes.
Happiness is riding my purple, Groovy Chick bike.
Happiness is when my cousin Natasha sleeps over at my house.
Happiness is when my brother is being funny and tickling me.
Happiness is when I am playing with my dolls.
Happiness is when I am bouncing on my bed.
Happiness is when I go to my uncle's.
Happiness is when I am playing on my trampoline with Chloe Willis.
Happiness is when I play games with my cousin on a Friday night.
Happiness is when I am in my bed reading the 'Ghost Teacher' book.
Happiness is when I am with my cousins Amy, Natasha
                                                    and Rachelle.
Happiness is when I am going to Granny's house.
Happiness is when it is my birthday.

Lois Glendinning (8)
Cookstown Primary School, Cookstown

Happiness Is . . .

Happiness is out in the back garden bouncing on my trampoline.
Happiness is when I'm watching the 'Suite Life of Zach and Cody'.
Happiness is spending time with my big sister and big brother
                                                    Robyn and Lee.
Happiness is when I see my great teacher, Miss Scott.
Happiness is when I have a sleepover at Bethany's or Chloe's house.
Happiness is when Bethany comes to my house and we go
                                                    on the swings.

Chloe McGuigan (7)
Cookstown Primary School, Cookstown

Happiness Is . . .

Happiness is going outside at lunchtime playing 'stuck in the mud'
with Ryan
Happiness is playing football on the beach with Lee.
Happiness is doing PE at school, playing races.
Happiness is watching the Twelfth, all the drummers, fluters
and flaggers.
Happiness is when I write a story on Friday after break time.
Happiness is seeing Ryan down the town.
Happiness is when I saw Miss Scott walking past the graveyard
with her dogs when I was coming home from Cookstown Youth.
Happiness is riding my bike.

Marc Glasgow (7)
Cookstown Primary School, Cookstown

Happiness Is . . .

Happiness is when I play teachers with my twin sister.
Happiness is when I go for a walk with my dog.
Happiness is when I can draw and colour at school.
Happiness is when I get to hold my sister's guinea pig and it squeaks.
Happiness is when I go to see my daddy.
Happiness is going shopping with Mummy and my twin sister.
Happiness is when I play games with my twin sister.
Happiness is when I go on my daddy's motorbike with him.
Happiness is when I go to the seaside with my mummy
                                                  and my twin sister.
Happiness is when I go to school.

Shalanda Shannon (7)
Cookstown Primary School, Cookstown

Happiness Is . . .

Happiness is looking forward to getting a goldfish on Thursday.
Happiness is going on holiday and playing in the sand.
Happiness is playing teachers with my friends and I am the teacher.
Happiness is when Auntie comes to stay with me for two days.
Happiness is when I stay with my auntie; we go up town and do
some shopping.
Happiness is when I read a book on a Saturday night.
Happiness is when I go to Parkanaur on a school trip.
Happiness is when I go to the swimming pool and I swim across.
the pool.
Happiness is when I go to the library with my daddy's sister.

Leah Anderson (8)
Cookstown Primary School, Cookstown

Happiness . . .

Happiness is when Man United wins a match.
Happiness is going to school.
Happiness is seeing our principal.
Happiness is seeing Miss Scott.
Happiness is getting toys.
Happiness is playing on the PlayStation.
Happiness is riding a bike.
Happiness is going to the circus.
Happiness is seeing my best friend Mathew Crook.
Happiness is when I read a book.
Happiness is drawing a picture.
Happiness is getting a golden badge.

Sam Purvis (8)
Cookstown Primary School, Cookstown

Happiness Is . . .

Happiness is playing football with my dad out in the back garden.
Happiness is riding my bike to the shop.
Happiness is getting my lunch of chicken sandwiches at lunchtime.
Happiness is when I learn to multiply in school.
Happiness is when I do my 500-metre badge in the swimming pool.
Happiness is when I try and catch butterflies in the back garden.
Happiness is when I watch TV in my bed, all snuggled up.

Adam Martin (8)
Cookstown Primary School, Cookstown

Happiness Is . . .

Happiness is when
I play with my friends
Happiness is when
I trick or treat at Hallowe'en
Happiness is when
I play football
Happiness is when
I eat a pizza
Happiness is when
I get sweets
Happiness is when
I write a poem
Happiness is when
I do well at school
Happiness is when
I go to the pool
Happiness is when
I go to the zoo
Happiness is when
I go to the shop
Happiness is when
I play with my toys
Happiness is when
I go to bed at the end of the day.

Cameron Mullan (8)
Cookstown Primary School, Cookstown

The Rifle

Ever since the rifle came
war and death has struck
it only brings bad tidings
and not a single piece of luck

But remember things like World War II
when many a good man died
but the rifle did help
the rest of us stay alive

So the rifle can be good
and also make us sad
it can fight for freedom
or hurt us really bad

Ever since the rifle came
I couldn't really decide
whether to embrace it
or run away and hide.

Tommy Kilpatrick (10)
Crosshouse Primary School, East Kilbride

Christmas

C hristmas is my favourite day,
H ot puddings sitting on the table!
R oasting in the oven
 I s lots of lovely food!
S anta's almost here,
T aking hold of the reins!
M unching cookies and drinking milk,
A nd coming down the chimney,
S anta's been and gone!

Kirsten Macaulay (10)
Crosshouse Primary School, East Kilbride

Clowns

Clowns are funny.
Clowns are fun.
Until that is, the party's done.
He doesn't get any pay,
For working all the party day.
Not to forget, without any pay,
For working his lungs off, blowing balloons all day.
And all the screeches,
And cries of all the children.
Without any pay, all day.
Poor clown!

Ian Lonsdale (10)
Crosshouse Primary School, East Kilbride

Hallowe'en

A dark scary night
Everyone giving me a fright
I go and ring the doorbell
I am a witch so I tell the lady a spell
But she is a witch too!
Boo!
But I'd just like to say
Hallowe'en is scary but I like it anyway.

Tegan Brodie (9)
Crosshouse Primary School, East Kilbride

Happiness

Happiness feels like fluffy clouds.
Happiness tastes like melted chocolate.
Happiness looks like sunshine.
Happiness smells like red roses.
Happiness reminds me of all my family!

Caitlin Abberley (10)
Crosshouse Primary School, East Kilbride

Summer

Summer is the time to have fun
Go to the beach and chill out
Go and have fun in the sun
Have fun with your family, go out and about
Don't stay inside all day
Go out and have fun
Have fun in the summertime.

Chloe Kennedy (10)
Crosshouse Primary School, East Kilbride

Hallowe'en

A dark scary night
With lights so bright
Ghosts and skeletons all around
Sometimes they make me fall to the ground
There are witches and ghosts everywhere
They give my brother a little scare
Hallowe'en is scary, I am sorry to say
But we all like it anyway.

Louise McFarlane (10)
Crosshouse Primary School, East Kilbride

Football

F ootball is the best.
O ne day I hope to be a professional player.
O ther teams' scouts will be around.
T rying out football boots.
B all control is fun.
A ll the players trying their hardest.
L istening to the shouts for a pass.
L istening to the coach.

Jack Reid (10)
Crosshouse Primary School, East Kilbride

The Crazy Relaxing Holiday

One bright morning in Corfu,
The sun was shining,
The birds were singing in some stupid languages,
A day of relaxation,
On the golden sand off the coast of Canal d' Amour.
The best Greek salad
Followed by a big juicy steak with chilli sauce on top
Or is it?
Yeah!
Watching an outstanding Greek night.
Fire dancing,
Plate smashing.
It just doesn't get any better.

Conor Smith (10)
Crosshouse Primary School, East Kilbride

Christmas

Christmas is my favourite day of the year
Hot turkey on the table
Roast potatoes ready to eat
In the oven is a Christmas treat
Sacks of presents ready to open
My stocking with lots of gifts
All of my favourite food
Santa with his red sleigh in the air.

Paige Matthews (10)
Crosshouse Primary School, East Kilbride

Porsche

I like Porsches, they are the best.
They have spoilers for drifting and turning.
They have big engines, as big as me!
They pump like a lion roaring.
Think how fast they go.
Red is the colour of my favourite machine.

Shaun McCann (9)
Crosshouse Primary School, East Kilbride

The Wolf

The wolf's eyes reflect the moonlight,
Its fur as soft as a newly bought rug.
It howls on the mountain in front of the moon,
Its furry shadow stands out as it calls,
In the winter moonlight.
Its head held up high,
Towards the dark night sky,
As it sits on the mountain in front of the moon.
When it runs, it hardly makes any noise,
You can only hear it softly padding through the snow.
The wolf is so strong, just like a very, very strong person.
The wolf is so fast, as fast as a cheetah,
Its leg joints are seen moving as it runs.
The wolf is also very beautiful, a rare and special species.
I love it so, and so do many other people.
The wolf is amazing, super-extraordinary,
That's why it's my favourite animal.

Jessica Lam (10)
Cwmclydach Primary School, Tonypandy

Rugby World Cup

Rugby World Cup
Twenty teams, four groups, who's in which?
New Zealand, the terrifying Haka
Against the almighty Portugal
The first match in the World Cup
Then a different match
France against Argentina, what an awesome match
The eightieth minute
Twelve-ten to France, penalty!
Argentina makes it thirteen-twelve
Argentina wins!
South Africa against England
The final crowd is going mad
England might have scored a try, not a try
Fans go quiet, they both have a penalty
Both make it!
South Africa has two penalties
They make it!
They win the World Cup trophy.

Curtis Povey (10)
Cwmclydach Primary School, Tonypandy

The Sun

The sun is like blazing hot flames.
It's like a fireball but it's about ten times larger.
The sun gleaming on the beach, heating it up.
It makes people happy when the sun is gleaming on the beaches.
Everyone is in love with the sun.
It is nice to look at it
But in space it is blazing hot.
I like the sun, it's pretty and beautiful and a little shiny.
The sun is very powerful with its hot blazing flames.

Henry Murphy (9)
Cwmclydach Primary School, Tonypandy

Can You Hear It?

Drip-drop, drip-drop
Can you hear it? Can you hear it?
Stomp, stomp, stomp, stomp.
Can you hear it? Can you hear it?
Can you feel it? Can you feel it?
Its scaly flesh flashing before you.
Can you hear it? Can you hear it?
Its loud powerful roar bearing its yellow teeth.
Can you see it? Can you see it?
Its red smoky eyes like two cigars.
Can you see it? Can you see it?
Its sharp claws, as long as its legs
Are hooked onto the floorboards.
Can you smell it? Can you smell it?
Its garlicky breath, although you can't feel it.
Can you hear it? Can you hear it
Clawing towards you?
Can you feel it? Can you feel it
Shaking the Earth?
Can you see it? Can you see it
Coming closer,

Anna-Rose Thomas (10)
Cwmclydach Primary School, Tonypandy

A Zombie

His round head is like a bowling ball.
His red eyes are like blood.
His rotten teeth are yellow as the bright sun.
His green, green, arms are as green as a spiked cactus.
His horrible feet, green skin peeling off like a curled rug.
His ears, with wax dripping from them, like a melting ice cream.
His mouth, dripping with blood like fire.
His belly is so skinny you can see his bones.

Jonathan Thomas (9)
Cwmclydach Primary School, Tonypandy

Pain

Pain feels like three hot irons are running through your head
Pain makes life bad and sad
Pain is freezing cold
Pain feels like a elephant crushing your legs
Pain is a message of broken bones and rushing blood
Pain feels like a bone has gone missing
Pain is life, everyone experiences it
Pain is even a graze or the tiniest bruise, it's still pain
Pain feels like your body can't move
Pain gives you needles and stitches
Pain makes everyone sad
Pain feels like a hot desert and days with no food or drink
And sometimes pain makes you see the light and die
And pain becomes your enemy
And everyone cries when you're dead in bed!

Kieran Thomas (10)
Cwmclydach Primary School, Tonypandy

The Sun

The sun has got balls of fire shooting from it
When I look at the sun I can see the balls shooting in the sky
And when I look at the sun it feels nice and warm on my face.

When I look at the sun, it makes me happy
Then I can go and play in the sun
Then I can take my jumper off
When I am in the sun I go red like a tomato
When I take off my sunglasses my eyes water
And it looks like I've been crying.

Lewis Thomas (9)
Cwmclydach Primary School, Tonypandy

A Windy Beach

A windy beach has windy waves
Smashing against the rocks
The wind whistles very, very loudly
And gushes through your hair.
The sand is flying in big, big heaps
Stinging your eyes when it hits them hard.
You can feel the sand hit your skin
Making it sting so badly.
It flies around your feet
Like lots of dogs running around
The only shelter, behind the rocks.
Sitting on the beach
The sand not stinging you now
Happy now at last!

Matthew Parsons (10)
Cwmclydach Primary School, Tonypandy

The Way Through Fright

You walk into a room
Your mind plays tricks on you
You think there is someone there
You hear noises
You hear footsteps
They start to get closer
You get ready
You start seeing
You run out of the room
And all the worry is over
You are huffing and puffing
But it is over!

Kyran Thomas (9)
Cwmclydach Primary School, Tonypandy

Sorrow

Sorrow is not calm
it feels like you're lonely,
but you're not.
Don't worry they will always believe in you
and be with you.

Sorrow is a hard time,
don't feel down.
They will watch you as time grows,
if you still love them,
they will still love you.

Sorrow is quiet now
the one you loved has gone,
you will see them soon
don't worry.

Sorrow can hurt but it will soon wear off
you will feel loved again.

Simone Thomas (10)
Cwmclydach Primary School, Tonypandy

Dogs

In the night the dogs sleep
In the afternoon the dogs are wide awake for opponents
At teatime they eat their food and are still awake
At night they are sleeping but one eye opens.

They are ready to pounce at any person
They hear footsteps, they run to the door
It's the postman, he posts two letters
And he or she tears and rips it in one go!

Nikita McCarthay (10)
Cwmclydach Primary School, Tonypandy

The Way Through A Teacher's Mind

Oh what lovely screaming kids
Playing in their yard
Having the time of their lives.
The bell goes, what a roar
The kids come rushing like elephants
So hungry for their food.
They eat their creamy dessert
They go out to play again
Playing all the rough games
They are answering back all the time.
I don't know who they think they are.
They all say they won't get hurt
Then the whole playground freezes.
Scream! Someone's been hurt!

Devon Howard (10)
Cwmclydach Primary School, Tonypandy

The Way Through Pain

The way through pain
Feeling it shooting up your legs
The blood running everywhere
Then your leg getting bigger and bigger.

It feels like someone is having a party in your leg
And they are just cutting the cake
The pain starts
The pain hurts
It does all different things
It can even kill
Sometimes it stings
It makes you bleed, it feels like you are dying
Your body turns and you start to scream!

Corey Thomas (10)
Cwmclydach Primary School, Tonypandy

Winter

As I walk through the door I feel cold air brush against my face.
I can hear the snow crunch beneath my feet
as I shuffle through the deep snow.
I see snowflakes fall from the sky,
as they catch the light, they shine like diamonds.
I see snowballs skim my face like bullets.
I feel something cold on the side of my head like ice,
where my friend has thrown a snowball at me.
My hat white where snow is falling on it,
my socks soaking where I've been in the snow,
it's like I've stepped into a deep pool of freezing cold water,
goose bumps on my arms because it is so cold.
I look up and see nothing but grey clouds stretching for miles.
The trees bare with no leaves just white from the freezing cold snow
as it still falls from the sky.
Then the sun breaks through and shines on me
like a light from Heaven.
It warms me like a fire burning, getting bigger and bigger.
The clouds come back over again and it gets cold.
Finally it gets dark and the street lights light up the snow.
I go inside my house,
I have a hot shower,
and then have a cup of tasty hot chocolate
sitting down on the sofa watching TV.

Adam Monaghan (11)
Cwmclydach Primary School, Tonypandy

The Sun

The sun shining down at my eyes so I can't see.
My skin as red as a beetroot.
As the sun is shining I run round the park happily playing.
Adults sunbathing and children having a lot of fun.

When I look at the sun my eyes water and it makes me happy.
The sun makes people have a lot of fun and play games in the park.

Shannon Webber (10)
Cwmclydach Primary School, Tonypandy

Football

The fans take their seats
There is a big cheer as the two teams come on the pitch
Kick-off is taken and the match starts
A player shoots but the keeper saves it, it's a corner
The ball is kicked in the box and is headed in
It's one goal to Manchester United
The whistle blows and it's half-time
The players have a rest and the fans go to the toilet
The match starts again
The opponents run down the field and are tackled
One player has to be stretchered off
Red card to Ferdinand, he's sent off!
The fans shout at the ref
The match ends at one-nil.

Rhys Thomas (10)
Cwmclydach Primary School, Tonypandy

The Sea On A Stormy Day

The sea is dark and grey,
And the waves splash fiercely.
The clouds are black and shooting with rain.
The sea smashes boats into pieces.
And forces people into the rocks.

Sometimes the sea can make whirlpools.
The whirlpools can suck boats underneath so they never get out.
Then after all that, it is nice and calm.
The sea is silent and peaceful.

Adrian Gerald Griffiths
Cwmclydach Primary School, Tonypandy

The Way Through Jamaica

The way through Jamaica,
all the people having fun,
loads of beautiful shops,
a beach like a hot desert,
the waves are beautifully calm like a smooth tower,
very lovely people playing and messing about.
Jamaica is exciting,
there is a lot of sport,
Jamaica is such a nice place, I could live here
the girls are wearing dresses,
the boys are in shorts.
A life in Jamaica is good.

Josh Edwards (10)
Cwmclydach Primary School, Tonypandy

The Way Through Pain

The way through pain is like iron shooting
into your knee,
the pain hurts badly
like a lion roaring with a sore leg.
The pain is severe with blood
dripping down your leg.
The pain really, really hurts.
With blood dripping down your leg
the crying from pain is bad.
When you start crying
you start screaming like a monkey.

Chloe Edwards (9)
Cwmclydach Primary School, Tonypandy

The Way Through A Forest

The way through a forest
is damp and wet and dark.
The road is covered in moss and roots
that stay beneath the ground waiting for water.
The trees are covering the sunlight.
When the night comes, creatures come out,
badgers, hedgehogs and deer
they all look for food to eat
and take home for the winter
When morning comes
there is a lot of snow on the trees.

Joel Shanley Davies (10)
Cwmclydach Primary School, Tonypandy

Cold

Cold feels horrible and miserable.
When I step off my doorstep
My hands start to freeze
And my toes are white and pale.
My hair is frozen like ice
And my ears are blocked rock-solid with ice.
When I walk to the shop
I can hardly move my feet and arms.
When I wake up in the mornings
I am very, very cold.
When I go out in the rain
It is very cold.

Corie Southwood (11)
Cwmclydach Primary School, Tonypandy

The Bonfire

The bonfire sparkled, flickered and boomed into the sky.
Red, orange and yellow flames swooshed to the sky.
Flames stretched into the dark eerie night.

The white, pale, gloomy moon was like a white ball
Shining from the black sky.
The moon crawled along the sky
Shining on everything it met.

Bursting, crackling, popping flames
Exploded up to the moon.
The smoke crawled to the glittery stars.

Witches swooshed around the bonfire
Cackling, swinging around, chanting their spells.

Rian McDaid (10)
Evish Primary School, Strabane

The Bonfire

The bonfire's flames flickered all through the eerie night
As the lonely silver plate sat down and started to frown.
The bonfire sizzled as the flames roared and flickered
As the wolves howled around the backdrop of the misty forest.
Wicked witches whirled around the multicoloured fire sniggering
And then turned around just before midnight.

Ryan Flanagan (11)
Evish Primary School, Strabane

Autumn

Autumn, you have come and chased Summer away
You make leaves flutter to the ground and form a blanket.
Howling winds whisper through your chimney.
Shiny brown conkers bombs to the ground.
Bare skeleton trees reaching to the dull sky.
Things slowing down, dark evenings, we huddle by the fire.
Hallowe'en's looking, witches come out at night.
Mother Nature has come and has given us a beautiful autumn.
Crispy golden leaves racing along the ground
Chasing signs of summer away . . .

Aoife Devine (10)
Evish Primary School, Strabane

Feelings

Anger:
Anger is madness
It is a lion's roar
Anger is a red-hot volcano bubbling hot
It is like a stampede of elephants
It feels like the wind.

Love:
Love is like a baby
It's like soft marshmallows
It is gentle and kind
It is caring
It is so nice and sweet
And makes you smile each day.

Seaghda Cullen (9)
Evish Primary School, Strabane

There's A Rainbow In My Garden

My creaky wooden fence,
as red as the petals on a red rose
or a hot fiery flame.

> My bluebells in the flowerbed
> as blue as the deep blue sea
> or the high-up sky.

My silky grass
as green as the leaves on the tree in summer
or someone's green eyes.

> My shiny metal watering can
> as yellow as the shimmering sun
> or the yellow brick road of the Wizard of Oz.

Loads of little butterflies
as purple as foxgloves
or ripe plums.

> My muddy soil
> as brown as wood
> or a stick insect.

My creepy-crawly minibeasts
as black as the midnight sky
or black, black hair.

> *There's a rainbow in my garden.*

Emily Davies (11)
Godre'rgraig Primary School, Godre'rgraig

There's A Rainbow In My Garden

There's a pile of leaves in my garden
as red as a little bit of blood
or as red as my homework book

There's a pond in my garden full of fish
as blue as the summer's sky
or as blue as the sparkling sea

There's a big patch of grass in my garden
as green as the trees in sunny places
or as green as broccoli

There's a big tall sunflower in my garden
as yellow as the shiny sun
or as yellow as a lemon

There's a lot of blackberries in my garden
as purple as some fresh grapes
or as purple as purple plums.

There's a pot full of soil in my garden
as brown as a bouncing brown bunny
or as brown as thick gloopy mud.

There's a spider in my garden
as black as the night sky
or as black as a cave full of darkness.

Eben Vaughan-Philipps (9)
Godre'rgraig Primary School, Godre'rgraig

There's A Rainbow In My Garden

A broken bucket
as red as a burning fire
or a brand new shiny car.

A lively pond
as blue as a sunny sky
or a blue tile in a swimming pool.

Loads of grubby weeds
as green as a springtime leaf
or a wet grass field.

A little welly
as yellow as the shiny sun
or Sahara desert sand.

A pufferfish
as purple as a pretty fuchsia
or a tall foxglove.

A plastic plant pot
as brown as a tree trunk
or a pot of shiny brown paint.

A dull trampoline
as black as a plain rubber tyre
or a blank computer screen.

There's a rainbow in my garden.

Lucy Griffiths (10)
Godre'rgraig Primary School, Godre'rgraig

The Rainbow In My Garden

There's a rainbow in my garden
a thin leaf
as red as a rose
or a shiny red apple.

A small sparkling bluebell
as blue as a blue tit
or a kingfisher.

A shiny shield bug
as green as a soft smooth leaf
or a thin piece of grass.

A crispy leaf
as yellow as moss
or a round juicy lemon.

A flowing foxglove
as purple as a fuchsia
or a sparkling petal.

A tall tree
as brown as a squirrel
or a huge log.

A long caterpillar
as black as mud
or a widow spider.

Joshua Hopkin (11)
Godre'rgraig Primary School, Godre'rgraig

There's A Rainbow In My Garden

There's a rainbow in my garden,

A scented rose in the soil
as red as a poppy's petal
or a fox's pelt.

A wooden bench ready to sit on
as blue as a bluebell
or a blue tit sitting on the fence.

Prickly holly bush leaves
as green as a shiny green apple
or silky green grass.

A daffodil as yellow as the burning sun
or a crispy autumn leaf.

A foxglove, lovely to look at
as purple as a fuchsia
or a fresh plum just picked from the bush.

A burnt mud soil waiting in the packet
as brown as the bark of a tree
or as rough as a hedgehog's spines

A warm black dog waiting for a walk
or as black as smoke coming from the chimney.

The rainbow in my garden!

Emilia Lawrence (10)
Godre'rgraig Primary School, Godre'rgraig

There Is A Rainbow In My Garden

An old muddy plant pot
as red as a warm winter's fire,
or a bright poppy in a field.

There is a wet, cold, watering can
as blue as a beautiful blue tit's feathers,
or a swaying bluebell in the wind.

There is a thick wet patch of grass
as green as a new leaf in the spring,
or a juicy green apple.

There is a yellow daffodil
shining in the sun like a star
or as yellow as a sandy beach.

There is a newly painted shed
with its paint glistening in the sun
with a view of purple mountains from the window.

There is a crumbling bench
as brown as friendly dog's ears
or a rabbit in its burrow.

There is an old, unwanted boot
as black as the night sky,
or a liquorice sweet.

The rainbow in my garden . . .

Aimee Lauren Jones (10)
Godre'rgraig Primary School, Godre'rgraig

There's A Rainbow In My Garden

There's a rainbow in my garden

A scarlet poppy
as red as a silky fox
or a shiny apple

A sparkling pond
as blue as a blue tit's feathers
or a brand new car

A shiny green shield bug
as green as a bright leaf
or a watery grass

A warm sun
as yellow as a lion
or a desert plain

A pretty fuchsia
as purple as a grape
or a shiny wet hippo

A creaky old shed
as brown as a grizzly bear
or crumbly soil

A small ant
as black as a dim light
or a cute black cat.

Liam James Walsh (10)
Godre'rgraig Primary School, Godre'rgraig

There's A Rainbow In My Garden

There's a rainbow in my garden
a freshly picked rose
as red as a big juicy apple.

There's a rainbow in my garden
a big bouncy ball
as blue as the ocean.

There's a rainbow in my garden
a field full of wavy grass
as green as a big frog.

There's a rainbow in my garden
a field of fresh daffodils
as yellow as the bright burning sun.

There's a rainbow in my garden
a beautiful round plum
as purple as a lovely-smelling iris.

There's a rainbow in my garden
a new garden shed
as brown as the bark on the tall trees.

There's a rainbow in my garden
an ugly crow
as black as the sparkling night sky.

Jo Diana Price (10)
Godre'rgraig Primary School, Godre'rgraig

There's A Rainbow In My Garden

A swaying bright poppy
as red as cherry tomatoes,
or a shiny fox's coat.

A big clear pool
as blue as the ocean sea,
or our school jumpers

The thick long grass
as green as a juicy lime,
or a crunchy cucumber

A beautiful daffodil
as yellow as the bright hot sun,
or a delicious banana.

An exotic delphinium
as purple as the morning sun,
or as juice as a vale of grapes.

Slimy thick mud
as brown as a soaring eagle,
or a lumpy slippery toad.

A scary, creepy spider,
as black as the night sky
or a gloomy dark hole in the wall.

I love my rainbow garden.

Chlöe Hughes (9)
Godre'rgraig Primary School, Godre'rgraig

There's A Rainbow In My Garden

Five beautiful red roses
as red as flames in snow
or the beautiful sunlight in the morning.

A deep pool
as blue as the beautiful blue sky
or the deep blue ocean.

A lovely greenhouse
as green as the shining grass
or the shiny leaf.

A painted yellow gate
As yellow as a yellow cute duck
or the shining sun.

A cute purple flower
as purple as purple tasty grapes
or poisonous foxgloves.

A beautiful brown old sunflower
as brown as an old tree's bark
or stick insects.

A disgusting black snail
as black as a big gorilla
or black as the dirty soil.

There's a rainbow in my garden

Suzie Chang (10)
Godre'rgraig Primary School, Godre'rgraig

There's A Rainbow In My Garden

A rose
as red as a poppy
or a ladybird,

A bluebell
as blue as a blue tit
or a gleaming ocean,

Grass
as green as moss
or seaweed,

A daffodil
as yellow as the sun
or a beautiful sunflower,

Foxgloves
as purple as grapes
or a blueberry,

Mud
as brown as soil
or tree bark,

A cat
as black as a blackbird
or a spider.

Georgia May Meyrick (10)
Godre'rgraig Primary School, Godre'rgraig

There's A Rainbow In My Garden

A berry bush
as red as a rose,
or a shiny red apple.

A tall bluebell
as blue as the bright sky,
or a fluffy bluebird.

A juicy pear
as green as tall trees,
or a freshly mowed grass.

A beautiful sunflower
as yellow as the sparkling sun,
or a round melon.

A lovely foxglove
As purple as a fresh plum,
or a purple flowerpot.

A creaking shed
as brown as a lively hedgehog,
or muddy soil.

A sparkling night
as black as a scary spider,
or a shiny bird table.

The rainbow in my garden.

Elisha Flack (10)
Godre'rgraig Primary School, Godre'rgraig

There's A Rainbow In My Garden,

A juicy, ripe apple
as red as a drop of blood,
or as a new blooming rose.

The wide sky above
as blue as feathers from a bluebird,
or a shining new plant pot.

The freshly cut grass
as green as a leaf falling from a tree,
or a weed growing very slowly.

A sunflower as tall as the clouds,
as yellow as the shining sun,
or the peel of a banana.

A fragrant iris, tall and sweet
as purple as juicy plums in summer,
or a purple small watering can.

New sweet-smelling potatoes rising from the soil
as brown as the bark from a tree,
or a new wooden shed.

A big, hairy, scary spider
as black as a slow, slimy slug,
or a creepy-crawly woodlouse.

There's a rainbow in my garden.

Abigail Zoe Jones (9)
Godre'rgraig Primary School, Godre'rgraig

There's A Rainbow In My Garden

An apple,
as red as a silky poppy petal
or a shiny letterbox.

A glistening raindrop,
as blue as ink
or a small bluebird.

A shiny leaf,
as green as grass
or a beautiful ripe pear.

A bright sunflower,
as yellow as the sun
or a ripe pepper.

A broken flowerpot,
as purple as a fuchsia
or a bird table.

An old shed,
as brown as soil
or some bark off a tree.

A cracked watering can,
as black as a berry
or a spider.

There's a rainbow in my garden.

Jessica Amber Danaher (9)
Godre'rgraig Primary School, Godre'rgraig

There's A Rainbow In My Garden

There's a red beautiful butterfly
as red as a roaring fire
or a poppy field.

There's a bluebell swaying in the wind
as blue as a crystal.

There's grass in my garden
shining in the sunlight
or green as a fresh leaf off a new tree.

There's some golden sand
glittering in the sun.

There's a lovely fuchsia in my garden
as purple as an onyx crystal.

There's a hedgehog sleeping peacefully in my garden
as brown as a prickly conker.

There's a badger in my garden making a home
as black as a jaguar.

There's a rainbow in my garden.

Ashley Clavey (11)
Godre'rgraig Primary School, Godre'rgraig

There's A Rainbow In My Garden

A colourful butterfly,
as red as a juicy shiny apple,
or as red as a rose.

As bright as the sun,
As blue as the sky
or a bluebird's feathers.

A shiny watering can
as green as long wavy grass
or a green bushy tree.

As bright as the sun
as yellow as the hot boiling sun
or a sunflower.

A big shed,
as brown as a slimy slug
or a woodlouse.

A flying fly,
as black as dirty soil
or a blackbird.

Carys Phillips (9)
Godre'rgraig Primary School, Godre'rgraig

There's A Rainbow In My Garden

A ripe apple
as red as a proud robin's breast.

A beautiful bird
as blue as the bright sky.

A bouncing slimy frog
as green as the blowing grass.

A lovely tall sunflower
as yellow as the burning sun.

A lovely purple ball rolling around the garden
as purple as a fresh plum.

My dark wooden shed
as brown as a burnt log.

A black slippery slug
as black as a tossing long worm.

Tamzin Diaper (9)
Godre'rgraig Primary School, Godre'rgraig

There's A Rainbow In My Garden

As red as a red juicy tomato
growing in my garden.

A shiny bluebird sitting on the fence.

The green grass waving in the field.

As yellow as a fresh banana shining in the garden
waiting to be eaten.

A purple bunch of grapes just lying there
like a fresh plum.

As brown as a shed
and like a new bench in the garden.

As black as the sky in the sparkling night-time.

Lauren Jones (9)
Godre'rgraig Primary School, Godre'rgraig

There's A Rainbow In My Garden

A shiny ladybird,
as red as a ripe apple,
or a fragrant rose.

A bluebird
as blue as the bright sky
or a cluster of pretty bluebells

A hopping frog,
as green as a beautiful lily pad
or some scrummy peas in a pod.

A yummy, scrummy banana
as yellow as the shining sun
or the soft desert sand

A gorgeous bowl of grapes,
as purple as some pretty foxgloves
in a bright forest
or a juicy plum.

A damp patch of soil,
as brown as some bark,
or a big splat of mud.

A *monstrous* scary spider,
as black as a shiny bird table,
or a noisy blackbird.

There's a rainbow in my garden.

Kasey-Jayne Counsell (10)
Godre'rgraig Primary School, Godre'rgraig

The Magic Horse

Once I saw a magic horse
Jumping a course
Then he came over to me
And made me hoarse.

I was shouting at him to slow down
Then he started to fly
I was so scared
He started to fly very high.

Then he shouted
'Hurry, we have to go!'
I ran and jumped on
Then he flew very low.

Naomi McConnell (9)
Gortin Primary School, Gortin

On The Mountain

A ram and a lamb
Were grazing on a mountain.
The sheep were watching
Over the fountain.

A very loud noise
Came rumbling by.
The sheep were so frightened,
They ran across the mountain.

Aaron McMullin (7)
Gortin Primary School, Gortin

Weather

On a windy day
The leaves
Flutter down from the tree
Like little helicopters flying in the sky.

On a sunny day
The butterflies
Come out to fly around and around
Like a kite in the sky.

On a rainy day
The rain
Falls down and batters the windows
Like bombs going off.

Alex Hempton (8)
Gortin Primary School, Gortin

Sounds I Like

Whistling of the wind in the morning
Crumpling of autumn leaves
Explosion of a bomb
Buzzing of a bee
Hooting of an owl
Squeak of a mouse
Crash of a car.

Scott McNally (7)
Gortin Primary School, Gortin

Autumn

The leaves raced each other along the track
Trees went to sleep
Trees waved their branches in the wind
Squirrel ate all her hidden nuts
The birds sang all day
Squirrels played in the autumn leaves
Autumn leaves danced in the sunshine.

Jacob McIlwaine (9)
Gortin Primary School, Gortin

Autumn Personified

Leaves dance in the wind,
Conkers glide to the ground in the wind,
The tree sleeps ready for the wintertime,
A conker sleeps in his spiky bed,
Squirrels play in the brown and orange leaves,
Wind runs towards the car,
The squirrel gathers all his nuts in the autumn time.

Andrew McFarland (9)
Gortin Primary School, Gortin

My Magic Box

I had a magic box
Inside it was a pig.
I opened it one day
And the pig began to jig.

It ran down the road
And after it I hurried.
I did not know what to do,
I was very worried.

Thomas McIlwaine (8)
Gortin Primary School, Gortin

Autumn

Brown and orange leaves danced in the wind
Leaves jogged along the pavement in the gentle breeze
Squirrels gathered up their food for a winter feast
Big old ash tree went for his winter sleep
Little chestnut slept in her prickly bed
The raindrops wept on the window sill
Brown chestnut like a little boy's eyes
Wind ran after the car down the lane.

Chloe Campbell (10)
Gortin Primary School, Gortin

My Daddy

He is a bright blue,
On a sparkling summer's day.
He's in a field of singing birds.
He is the summer daylight,
In a stripy shirt and dark blue trousers.
He is a comfortable soft sofa.
He is an episode of Emmerdale,
He's a Galaxy chocolate bar.

Emily Pinkerton (9)
Gortin Primary School, Gortin

My Daddy

He is a silver star
Shining in the autumn sky.
Like a hurricane on the motorway
On a thundery day.
He is a leather bike suit.
Lying on a soft sofa.
Watching Emmerdale.
He is a juicy T-bone steak!

Zara Donnell (10)
Gortin Primary School, Gortin

Autumn

The deciduous trees slept in the cold winter nights,
Slender trees grew taller from year to year.
Autumn leaves danced in the chilly breeze,
A large conker slept in her spiky shell.
A beautiful thick cloud wore a sad face.
The squirrels ran about looking for fat nuts to eat.
The pretty starry night looked down.
The leaves wore beautiful shiny yellow or red coats,
The fat hedgehog crawled along the ground.
The field breathed quietly all night long under a new moon.

Aimee Porter (9)
Gortin Primary School, Gortin

My Auntie Dorothy

She is a lilac purple
Like the snow in winter,
She is a calm wave on the beach
Like the rain falling from the sky,
A warm soft jumper
Sitting on the sofa
Watching Coronation Street
A big packet of Maltesers.

Joshua Godber (10)
Gortin Primary School, Gortin

My Dog Sasha

She is a bright blonde
she is the summer
curled up in her bed
she is a warm coat
she is my warm soft armchair
a star in my eyes
and a hot apple pie, warm and sweet.

Nadine Kilpatrick (10)
Gortin Primary School, Gortin

Happiness Is . . .

When my mum smiles at me
A red sky
A bag of sweeties
When I feel special
Laughter
When I see my friends
Singing and dancing
A cosy bed
Christmas carols
Snow on the ground
Strawberries and cream
Birthdays, Christmas and holidays
Hot chocolate
Walking in crisp autumn leaves.

Jade Burns (9)
Greenhills Primary School, Glasgow

Happiness Is . . .

A big smile
Christmas trees
A bar of yummy chocolate
Being special
Watching fireworks
A friendly dolphin
A hug
A baby elephant
My new baby
Discovery television
A Nintendo Wii
A red rose
Trick or treating
Friends in school.

James McCann (10)
Greenhills Primary School, Glasgow

In My Dreams

I saw three mountains, one of ice, one of fire and one of thunder,
I saw a thundercloud, snow cloud and a fire cloud,
Yet they did not rain down,
I saw a rock that could move,
I saw a raging river stay still,
I saw a fire but it was cold,
I saw a white rainbow, no colour at all,
I saw a fox with nine tails,
I saw a clock that asked for the time,
I saw a dream world unfold.

Ryan Auld (10)
Kildrum Primary School, Cumbernauld

In My Dreams

I saw a runner with no supper
I saw a star that didn't shine
I saw a man doing a crime
I saw a dog that couldn't walk
I saw a river of hot chocolate
I saw Mark out of Smart hating Smart
I saw a fox that could talk
I saw a box that could box
I saw a shark that could bark
I saw a gran doing back flips
I saw a fan that made you warm
I saw a farm that had no barn
I saw a cat that could roar
I saw a crow crashing into a UFO.

Declan Cameron Murphy (10)
Kildrum Primary School, Cumbernauld

In My Dreams

I saw a dragon that couldn't breathe fire,
I saw chocolate sauce in the River Nile,
I saw a boy who was half-crocodile,
I saw a vampire with a broken tooth,
I saw a tiger lie down and woof,
I saw a thing called a Boingy-o-oof,
I saw a man run 2000 miles,
I saw Spider-Man stick to some tiles,
I saw a Dalek listening to rock,
I saw an eel in a cardboard box,
I saw a place where there was never any chickenpox,
I saw a bomb blow a cake up,
I heard my mum shouting, 'Cameron, time to get up!'

Cameron McTavish (9)
Kildrum Primary School, Cumbernauld

In My Dreams

I saw a dog with no legs.
I saw an elephant up in the blue sky.
I saw a bird that couldn't fly.
I saw a man who had no eye.
I saw a bus made of chocolate.
I saw a rat chasing a rat.
I saw a bee that couldn't see.
I saw a clock that asked the time.
I saw a granny doing a cartwheel.
I saw a deer drinking beer.

Sarah Louise Bergin (10)
Kildrum Primary School, Cumbernauld

Emotions

It feels like someone tickling you on the neck,
It is a bright yellow colour,
It tastes like a lovely cool ice cream,
It smells of fresh baked bread,
It looks like a lovely flower garden,
It sounds like a fun kids' party,
It is . . .
Happiness!

Kayleigh Armstrong (9)
Kildrum Primary School, Cumbernauld

Love

Love is a mixed red and pink colour,
Love tastes like a big bag of cotton candy,
Love smells like a bouquet of roses,
Love looks like millions of heart-shaped cards,
Love sounds like the cheers of a happy couple,
Love feels like the touch of a baby's finger.

Sarah Thornton (9)
Kildrum Primary School, Cumbernauld

Love

Love is pink like salmon from the sea,
It tastes like Belgian truffles,
It smells of beautiful red roses,
It looks like the fresh flowers in the countryside,
It sounds like happiness and joy,
Love feels like the most beautiful thing in the whole world!

Michael Mallinder-Macleod (10)
Kildrum Primary School, Cumbernauld

My Emotion

It is a warm red colour
It tastes like a hot cup of tea on a cold winter's night
It smells like a bed of red roses
It looks like a cosy bath with scented candles
It sounds like the laugh of a young baby
I feel this when I am with you
I feel *love*.

Rebekah L Lindsay (10)
Kildrum Primary School, Cumbernauld

Anger Is . . .

Anger is what I hate

Anger is black as a devil's heart
Anger tastes like rotten fruit
Anger feels like a bully in your head
Anger smells like a damp cellar
Anger looks like ice-cold water
Anger sounds like an evil laugh . . .

Andrew King (10)
Kildrum Primary School, Cumbernauld

Anger

Anger is a deep dark red,
Anger tastes like very heavy fire,
Anger smells like smoke,
Anger looks like it is thunder and lightning,
Anger sounds like hurting someone,
Anger feels like a bomb in my head!

Darren Aitken (10)
Kildrum Primary School, Cumbernauld

My Emotion

It is a cosy red colour
It tastes like a warm Sunday roast
It smells like a scented candle
It looks like a bed of roses
It sounds like a calm ocean abroad
It makes me feel like this . . .
When I'm in love.

Misha Davidson (10)
Kildrum Primary School, Cumbernauld

Emotions

It is a very hot colour,
It is hotter than Hawaiian beaches,
It smells like fire,
It looks like the Devil taking a life,
It sounds like horror,
It feels like punching someone in the face,
It is *anger!*

Alan Symington (10)
Kildrum Primary School, Cumbernauld

Emotions

It is like a red-hot fire,
It tastes like a rotten apple,
It smells like something has died,
It looks like a volcano erupting,
It feels like you are getting into a fight,
It is *anger!*

Sean Mendelovitch (10)
Kildrum Primary School, Cumbernauld

In My Dreams

I saw James Bond without a gun,
I saw a light but no sun,

I saw an apple that was gold and blue,
I saw a frog kiss a kangaroo!

I saw a dodo that could fly,
I saw a goat making apple pie,

I saw a tree that was growing money,
I saw bees that didn't like honey,

I saw a giant running sweet,
I saw a fish with stinky feet.

I saw a pond that was full of goo,
.I saw a flying bowling shoe,

I saw a party in the jungle,
I saw a rabbit that could only mumble,

I saw a monkey, 'Hello,' it said,
I saw an alarm clock and woke up in bed!

Stuart Boyce (10)
Kildrum Primary School, Cumbernauld

In My Dreams

I saw a man with no eye
I saw an elephant up in the sky
I saw a chocolate tree
I saw a bus that was made of honey you see
I saw a monkey swinging on a swing
I saw a bird without any wings
I saw a frog that couldn't hop
I saw a cat with a mop
I saw a monkey buying ice cream, it took a big lick
I saw a clock that couldn't tick
I saw a bee that couldn't sting
I saw a fox that could sing.

Antonia Brodie (10)
Kildrum Primary School, Cumbernauld

Country Lights

The fire looks like
Twinkling stars.
The rays of the moon
Blaze their light
Across the fields
Making everyone
Happy.

Inside the
Farmer's lamp
Two fireflies
Dancing to the
Click of his stick
Happily.

The moon
Is like a
Searchlight
Looking for the sun
Daily.

Daniel Thomas (10)
Llanedeyrn Primary School, Llanedeyrn

Country Lights

The farmhouse glows
The scramblers' lights are like balls of fire.
The campers' fire makes the fields glow
While the campers sing.
Tractors drive past working and digging
The lights are like moles' eyes.
A mole digging and ploughing
The indicators are winking at the people.
The moon gives light over the mountains and horizon.

Callum Jennings
Llanedeyrn Primary School, Llanedeyrn

Country Lights

The campfire dances
As the campers sing,
The moon is a shining torch
Giving light to others,
Stars are looking at me
Blinking as I walk through the fields,
As the night grows deeper
Tractor's gleaming eyes
Staring at me,
The farmhouse is pouring out its light
Spilling its juice all over the fields,
Scramblers with tiny lanterns
Bobbing on the end of the engines
Every day, every night.

Adele O'Sullivan (10)
Llanedeyrn Primary School, Llanedeyrn

Country Lights

The scramblers' engine groans loudly
The headlights look angry.
The farmhouse is lit up like a star.
The campers' fire dances when they're singing.
The tractor's light looks like a cat's eye
Looking for rat holes
The sunlight looks like a light bulb
Flicked on by God
The lanterns look like animals' eyes
Looking for food.

Farid Rashid (10)
Llanedeyrn Primary School, Llanedeyrn

What Will I Be When I Grow Up

What will I be when I grow up?
To be a bin man would be bad luck!
An optician, a vet, an architect or what?
I could be someone organised and do things on the dot.
How can I choose? There's so much to do.
I could be famous or be on TV
Or I could get a job in chemistry.
A banker, a businessman, a builder or what?
I could be an explorer and explore where it's hot.
To be an athlete would be fun, for miles and miles I would run.
A poet, a writer or an author, they are jobs like no other.
I could be an artist since I like to draw.
I would like to do something to do with the law.
A chef, a chiropodist, a carer or what?
I could be a doctor and tell sick people what they have caught.
What will I be when I grow up?
I think I'll be an architect.

Callum Forrester (11)
Miltonbank Primary School, Glasgow

The Troll

T errifying troublesome troll
H asty, hungry and horrible
E vilest mind in the universe

T oothless mouth covered in warts
R agged clothes and hairy feet
O ld and grey but very lively
L arge appetite for meat and liver
L egs are short but mouth is gushing.

Morgan Thomas (8)
Our Lady of the Angels RC School, Old Cwmbran

The Magic Box

(Based on 'Magic Box' by Kit Wright)

I will put in the magic box
A clown wearing a business suit throwing pies at Mr James.

I will put in the magic box
A dolphin from the finest sea.

I will put in the magic box
A blue dragon that breathes crystal ice.

I will put in the magic box
A mermaid with an electric tail.

My box is made of
The waves of the bluest sea with golden thread.

In my box I will
Turn into a mermaid and swim with the dolphins
And have adventures in the blue sea.

Elizabeth Earthey (9)
Our Lady of the Angels RC School, Old Cwmbran

The Troll

T errible teeth in his mouth.
H airy hair on his horrible head.
E vil ears covered in moles.

T errifying black mouth which eats children.
R ough skin and an orange tongue.
O ld neck which moves.
L ittle black eyes.
L onely, poor troll.

Lily Rafter Ambrosen (7)
Our Lady of the Angels RC School, Old Cwmbran

The Living Words

See the foggy mist that blinds your way
See the smoky fire that spits out the ashes
See the clear sunshine that lights up all your day.

Feel the sticky toffee that gets stuck in your teeth
Feel the prickly cactus that's dying in the sun
Feel the breezy wind of a spring day.

Hear the click of a clothes peg
Hear the banging of a bell
Hear the crunching leaves on an autumn day.

Taste the creamy yoghurt that stirs off the pot
Taste the salty sea of a beach
Taste the sun sweet berries of the earth.

Smell the sweet and sour lemon
That drips from the fridge.

Jacob McMorrow (10)
Our Lady of the Angels RC School, Old Cwmbran

The Magic Box

(Based on 'Magic Box' by Kit Wright)

I will put in the magic box
Beautiful butterflies by Botswana.
I will put in the box
The sweet smell of summer flowers.
I will put in the magic box
A moving mammal in the jungle.
I will put in the magic box
A magical making motivating mirror.
My box is made of
Ancient Greek magic and fresh cut grass.
In my box I will
Hold ancient Greek magic.

Huw Powell (9)
Our Lady of the Angels RC School, Old Cwmbran

Words That Live

See the dewy raindrops nestling on the lily pads.
See the blinding lights lighting up the land.
See the golden coins at the end of a stretching spectrum.

Feel the crumbling biscuits broken in half.
Feel the prickly cactus in the Arizona desert.
Feel the squidgy sponge in the bathtub.

Hear the sizzling sausage frying in the pan.
Hear the clanging boomerang flying in a circle.
Hear the banging fireworks on a November night.

Taste the creamy korma melting in your mouth.
Taste the salty water after you've been swimming.
Taste the sweet sugary lace as you swallow it.

Smell the scented candle burning brightly.
Smell the smoky fire as it curls up in flames.

Christiana Sturch (10)
Our Lady of the Angels RC School, Old Cwmbran

The Troll

T errible teeth munch and crunch.
H orrible eyes peeping at you.
E vil face, mouth hungry.

T errifying troll sleeps on your bones.
R ough body, skin slimy.
O ld face which is evil.
L arge feet, green and smelly.
L oves to eat people.

Bethany Smith (9)
Our Lady of the Angels RC School, Old Cwmbran

Autumn Colours

Autumn colours are like
The lovely jewellery that I wear to a disco,
The blazing fire in my living room,
The coloUful red boots that I wear to a party,
The bright wintry clothes I wear at Christmas,
The colourful rainbow that I see on showery days,
The pumpkins that we light at Hallowe'en,
The fireworks we light at Hallowe'en,
The Hallowe'en costumes we wear for trick or treating,
The beautiful hairbands I wear,
The beautiful bobbles I wear.

Ann McGarvey (9)
St Brigid's Primary School, Cranagh

Autumn Colours Are Like . . .

Autumn colours are like . . .
The leaves which make our world more colourful,
The beautiful rainbow which shines on us,
The gorgeous sunset.

Michael McMullan (8)
St Brigid's Primary School, Cranagh

Autumn Colours Are Like . . .

Autumn colours are like . . .
A fire in my living room,
My daddy's van,
My aunty's house,
My red coat,
My daddy's coat.

Stephen McGarvey (8)
St Brigid's Primary School, Cranagh

Autumn

Autumn colours are like . . .
The bright, warm clothes that I wear in the winter,
The hot, blazing fire in my living room on a cold evening,
The beautiful, bright colours of the rainbow,
The colourful flowers in my garden,
The colourful fireworks that go off at Hallowe'en,
The amazing colours of the sun setting,
The wonderful colours of my Hallowe'en costume,
The wonderful mountains,
The excellent colours on my sparkly necklace,
The bright colours on the computers.

Orla Kennedy (8)
St Brigid's Primary School, Cranagh

Autumn

Autumn colours are like . . .
The blazing fire outside the house,
The sunset at the seaside,
The delightful colours of a robin,
The pretty colours of my dog Glen,
The gorgeous leaves falling off the trees,
The shops which light up in autumn colours.

Emma McCullagh (9)
St Brigid's Primary School, Cranagh

Autumn

Autumn colours are like . . .
The brown leaves,
My red T-shirt,
My red pencil case.

Owen Conway (10)
St Brigid's Primary School, Cranagh

Autumn Colours Are Like . . .

Autumn colours are like . . .
The blazing red fire in my living room on a cold, dark
                                        winter's evening,
The brown, rough bark on the smooth tree,
The red breast of a robin singing its heart out,
My kitten, Rose, with her fur of brown and golden colours,
The brown and golden colours of a squirrel's fur shining in the sun,
The yellow rays of the sun shining down on us,
The orange pumpkin at Hallowe'en, glowing like it's alive inside,
The bright red apples ready to be bought,
The brown hot chocolate waiting to be drunk out of the cup,
The brown leaves crunch under my feet when I step on them,
The brown coats and yellow gloves ready to be bought and worn,
The red and brown bobbles I wear in my hair.

Hannah McMullan (9)
St Brigid's Primary School, Cranagh

Autumn Colours Are Like . . .

Autumn colours are like . . .
My daddy's red van,
The orange sunset that goes over my house,
Two of my imaginary friend's hair,
Lovely green grass around me,
My favourite colours.

Brónach Falls (8)
St Brigid's Primary School, Cranagh

Autumn

Autumn colours are like . . .
The fire that burns in our living room on a winter's day,
The beautiful flowers that grow in our garden,
The clothes that we wear in winter,
The sun that shines in through our windows,
The pictures that we painted,
The lovely mountains in the countryside,
The fireworks at Hallowe'en,
Our shiny shoes,
My dad's red car,
The colours on the computer,
The beautiful rainbow that shines on us,
Our yellow church beside our school.

Leanne McCrory (8)
St Brigid's Primary School, Cranagh

Autumn Colours Are Like . . .

Autumn colours are like . . .
A blazing fire in our living room on a cold winter's evening,
My kitten Rose, fur all orange and brown,
A blazing bonfire on Guy Fawkes' Night,
A pumpkin all orange and bright with yellow eyes,
A bright red strawberry in summer being picked,
A light brown squirrel getting ready for hibernation,
My dark brown hair during the day.

Kelly McMullan (11)
St Brigid's Primary School, Cranagh

Autumn Colours Are Like . . .

Autumn colours are like . . .
The sun setting over the great blue sea,
The blazing fire in my living room on a winter's evening,
The disco lights on a disco night,
The brown hawk flying in circles in the dark blue sky,
The autumn clothes in the shops for sale,
The sweetie wrappers when we go trick or treating,
The yellow sun shining over us,
The colours of the rainbow.

Roisin McAneney (9)
St Brigid's Primary School, Cranagh

Autumn

Autumn colours are like . . .
The burning fire in my house on a winter's day,
The beautiful mountains,
The beautiful disco lights,
The lovely sun,
The fireworks which go off at Hallowe'en,
The Ireland flag which is very colourful,
The colour of the lovely green fields.

Aine Bradley (8)
St Brigid's Primary School, Cranagh

Autumn

Autumn colours are like . . .
A fire in my living room,
Sparkling jewellery in the sun,
My shoes sparkling in the sun,
A beautiful rainbow,
The beautiful sun,
Hallowe'en fireworks.

Eunan Conway (8)
St Brigid's Primary School, Cranagh

Granda Fleming

I never got to meet you or your grave
But Dad said that you were really brave.
You loved your family, you loved your friends,
One day I'll come and meet you again.

Saw you in the photographs,
Long beard, looked like my dad.
He's got two kids now, me and my brother Paul.
We think about you when we're really sad.

I miss you loads.
I know you're dead but you still live in my heart
And in my head.

I miss you always.
You would've been so proud of me and my dad.

Eve Taylor-Fleming (10)
St Catherine's Primary School, Glasgow

I Miss You Granny

I miss you Granny,
Now that you're gone.
Even though it's
Been so long.

That day I saw you,
Carried down the aisle.
The length it took,
Seemed like a mile.

I know you're close,
But you seem so far away.
And I think you should know,
That I remember you each day.

Goodbye Granny,
As I weep beside your grave.
I'll miss you Granny,
Farewell, until the day.

Monica Hewitt (10)
St Catherine's Primary School, Glasgow

When You Passed Away

I was kneeling beside your bed,
Observing your stony, pale face.
Your frail fingers slid into mine,
Gripping me tight.

One single, silver tear toppled from your eyelashes
And fell down your pearly-white cheek.
You mumbled something, barely more audible than a whisper,
'Don't forget me!'

And your eyes fastened gently,
I whispered your name, getting more agitated by the second.
I screamed your name, tears plunging
And toppling down my cheeks.

'Nooo!' I cried, I could not take what was happening,
I didn't want to leave your side.
I felt hollowed as if something had gone
I could not replace.

I sank down to the carpeted floor, feeling limp and helpless.
My lip was trembling violently,
Tears pouring down my cheeks,
I felt totally deflated.

Feeling in a terrible and agitated state,
I screamed your name,
Almost pleading.

But no matter how loud I screamed,
No matter how many times I said your name,
Your eyes did not open,
Your limp body did not stir.

I gently said, (now knowing it was no use)
'I won't forget you,'
And I never have.

To this day I still have nightmares about that dreadful, sorrowful day.
At night I can't help calling your name,
Even though I know you won't answer
And of course you don't.

I felt this was unfair,
Even though I knew you were in a happier place
And were safe and looking down on me,
But I could not help feeling that you belonged here beside me.

And why did you have to go just yet,
Why couldn't you stay longer?
And I must tell you nothing has been the same,
Nothing has been right,
Since you passed away.

Sarah Kelly (11)
St Catherine's Primary School, Glasgow

When You're Here

When you're here, when I'm gone,
Don't forget to sing me a song.
In the time you think I'm dead,
Think of something else instead.

In the past you were strong.
We were always there.
Now if you work hard,
You can fight it alone.

We were always there, like your teddy bear.
We work as hard,
Just the same as you.
So don't dare say that you are to blame.

Amanda McMillan (10)
St Catherine's Primary School, Glasgow

The Final

St Catherine's Vs St Paul's at St Rock's Junior Park,
We went out to do our warm-up,
We all wanted to make our mark,
The kick-off was at half six,
Our emotions were a mix.
Half-past six fast approaching,
We were desperate to play,
This is the moment we were waiting on all day.

At half-time we rested our weary legs,
They were shaking so badly they felt like pegs.
As second-half kicked off we went right on the attack,
We scored within ten minutes, the defence was slack.

Declan was the goal scorer, we were all ecstatic,
But unfortunately they got a penalty,
We prayed for the ball to move like elastic.
We waited in long anticipation,
For the worst preparing.

Then all you heard was a big roar,
Lubo wasn't going to let them score.
Everyone thought it was our game,
St Paul's scored, we hung our heads in shame.

In the dying seconds of the match
St Paul's were awarded a free-kick.
Never before have I felt so sick.
Everyone moved out of the box and roared offside,
But the referee played on . . .
They scored, but we would not hide.

Suddenly the whistle blew, that's when everyone knew game over,
Everyone resting their weary legs.
I can't believe how disappointed I felt,
It was a complete disgrace.

Everyone stormed into the dressing room,
Not wanted to accept our medals.
Forced to watch St Paul's lift the cup,
But we have better respect than that,
We walked out with our heads held up.

As we accepted our medals we congratulated the opposition,
A hard decision when they displayed such egotism.

As soon as they lifted the cup
Our full team burst into tears,
The night turned out to be one of our worst fears,
But with honour and pride I dried my eyes,
Next year Khal Cullen refuses to cry.

Khal Cullen (11)
St Catherine's Primary School, Glasgow

Wish You Were Here Today!

Every time I think of you I cry.
I know I wasn't there for you all the time.
If I could turn the clock back I would,
To spend more time with you.

I look at the stars and see your face,
Wishing you were here today.
In the morning I woke and found you,
Dead in your bed in your room.

I felt like my life was ruined.
My soul was crushed.
My life would never be the same again.

A flitter of light and a drop of rain.
I will never forget about you.
I hope I will find the strength to carry on,
To live my life the way I did when you were here.

Hopefully I'll see you in Heaven,
With all the angels and saints.
Wishing you're here today,
Instead of all the pain and misery.

You were the *best,*
And you beat all the *rest.*
Rest in peace and be happy
Forever and ever.

Caragh Foreman (11)
St Catherine's Primary School, Glasgow

You Are Gone, I Miss You!

Sitting at your bedside,
I saw you there,
You couldn't even make it down the old patterned stair,
You were sick
And very thin,
You were frail and had pale skin.

Now you're gone,
I miss you loads,
I remember the white van you drove on the roads,
At your funeral I was crying,
My face was filled with a stream of tears,
In my dreams I still have fears.

On this day I remember you still,
I will always remember you,
I will, I will,
The day of your funeral,
I dreaded the moment
That your coffin left the church,
Hearts were breaking, people were crying,
My stomach began to lurch.

I was sad,
Also I felt bad,
I didn't feel so well,
You had cancer,
I know you did, and then I fell,
On my knees I started to pray,
For you to come back, but you were far away.

Now you're gone, reunited with your wife,
I have tried to forget that sorrowful day,
The day you lost your life.

I wish you were still here, to live one hundred years.

Until we meet again dear Uncle,
Until we meet again.

Cassie McAveety (10)
St Catherine's Primary School, Glasgow

Unforgettable Past

It was 2001, coming back from school,
My mum said, 'We're going to the hospital.'
Frozen in my car seat,
Not even daring to ask why.

As we wandered into the hospital
I asked my mum, 'Why?'
She didn't reply.
A gloomy nurse led us into a ward,
Lying in a hospital bed
Was my poor 68-year-old gran,
Lying painfully and motionless,
As anyone would be after a heart attack.

I grabbed her hand in mine and said,
'It's okay, you'll be fine.'
For days and days we visited,
Thinking hopefully every time.
To my own gran I wrote a thoughtful rhyme
As if her heart was beating to the time of mine.
The time, the place, it was all fitting in,
I said to my gran, 'You will pull through, I know it.'
Days and days passed and gran was recovering slowly.
I kept praying that she would recover quickly.
She soon recovered and now she is happy.
She hasn't fallem since 2001,
My gran is still my number one.

Fiona Gavin (10)
St Catherine's Primary School, Glasgow

She Is Coming Back, Isn't She?

The boy lost his mother that sorrowful day,
There was chaos through the night,
And screaming all around,
Some idiots set the fire off,
But were nowhere to be found.

Loads of precious lives were lost,
To the blazing fire,
Including a mother of one child,
He did not realise her loss.

He understood the fact that the fire should not be touched,
Although he didn't understand that she was never coming back.
'My mother is coming out here soon,'
Against that he would not stand,
But on the cold, lonely runway of truth,
Soon he would have to land.

They did not want to break it,
To the poor, now orphan boy,
Although the painful truth was told,
He did not get the meaning of death.

'I know she's gone but she is coming back,
She is coming back, isn't she?
I need my mum, I need her now.'
Remember he was only three.

Before the lot could stop him,
He went off like a shot,
Into the fire to join his mother,
And live with her for evermore.

Erin Nelson (11)
St Catherine's Primary School, Glasgow

When You Left

When you left I was broken,
Broken, never to be fixed.
When you left I was devastated,
Doomed to be eternally miserable.
All joy was gone
And you gone, never to come back.

My life was at an end,
You had left, leaving nothing but memories.
I call on those memories every day,
Hankering you'd come back.

When you left, I felt meaningless
And nothing could replace you.
Tears of sadness rolled down my face,
I didn't even dry them away.
You left, I was lost, you left, I was lost,
You were my guide, but now you're gone.

When you left, my nightmares haunted me,
I cried when I was wallowing in self-pity.
I would call for you,
But you never answered.
I needed you but you were never there.
'Help me, help me,' I whispered.
My heart called for you, my soul pleaded,
You never came.

When you left,
My heart screamed, cried, pleaded and wept.
When you left, I was depressed,
I never left the house.
I had no one to reassure me,
Where had you gone?

When you left, my world crumbled.
Why did you leave?
No hellos, no goodbyes,
No goodnights, no good mornings,
Just the wind on my face from an open window.

Kayrene Donnelly (11)
St Catherine's Primary School, Glasgow

Granny Rosie

Granny Rosie I try not to weep,
At night-time I cannot sleep,
It's not the same without you here,
I hope you are still very near.

Granny Rosie I love you so,
I really didn't want you to go,
I wonder why God choose you,
I hope you're looking down on everything I do.

I miss the way we played in the snow,
I really, really miss you, oh,
You are the night-time stars that glow,
I can remember your last words.

Especially when I hear those singing birds,
You are still here forever in my heart,
It's very hard to try and have a fresh start,
You are the best you know you are.

You're very sweet and one bright star,
I love you and you love me,
I know we will be together,
Now and forever.

D'Arcy Robertson (11)
St Catherine's Primary School, Glasgow

Football

Football feels like winning the Champions League
Football feels like being on my quad
Football feels like eating chocolate
Football feels like playing with my dog
Football feels like playing for Celtic and beating Rangers
2-0 in the Champions League Final.

Jordan Pirrie (8)
St Helen's Primary School, Condorrant

High School Musical!

High School Musical is really great
I watched it till very late
Gabriella is really quite small
Troy just loves to play basketball
Sharpay is always very moody
Ryan can be quite groovy
Sing and dance to the beat
And if you like get up on your feet
When High School Musical 2 comes out
You will hear me scream and shout!

Stephanie Cairney (9)
St Helen's Primary School, Condorrant

I Love Sports

S wimming is the best, my favourite stroke is breast
P laying and running to school is great, so go, don't be late
O rienteering is cool, I remember doing it at school
R ounders, what fun, you really need to run
T ennis with a bat and ball, what is your favourite of all?

Morgan Dillon (8)
St Helen's Primary School, Condorrant

Happiness

Happiness smells like the grass.
Happiness looks like the sun.
Happiness sounds like children playing.
Happiness reminds me of my mum and dad.

Robyn Kerins (9)
St Helen's Primary School, Condorrant

Animals, Dogs And Cats

A nimals are cute and cuddly,
N ever in the place you want them to be.
I nterested in their next meal,
M eat, meat they love to eat.
A lways wanting walks,
L ove to play and never bored.
S ome are big, some are small. I don't care I love them all.

Mark Beaton (9)
St Helen's Primary School, Condorrant

Candy

Candy is sweet, candy is nice
And candy is the sweet smell of sugar and spice.
Candy is blue, candy is red,
It tastes even better just before bed.
Candy is big, candy is small,
It doesn't matter to me, I like them all.

Joanne McLaren (9)
St Helen's Primary School, Condorrant

Love!

L ove is red when the sky is blue
O ver the moon I fly like a bird
V ery happy when I say the word love
E veryone is happy because of love.

Shannon McAuley (9)
St Helen's Primary School, Condorrant

Hallowe'en

Hallowe'en is finally here,
Monsters shouting trick or treat
Give us some sweets.
People singing poems besides homes.
Hallowe'en is the time of year
Where your peer
And scare with your friends!

Nathan Gallagher (10)
St John the Baptist Primary School, Roscor

Autumn

Autumn is here and leaves fall down
And children all begin to frown.
Summer is now over, it's back to school
And all the kids say boo school.
But never mind, Hallowe'en is here,
You better watch out, you might disappear!

Aisling Maguire (10)
St John the Baptist Primary School, Roscor

My Dad

Monster cutter
Expert boner
Careful vacuum packer
Nicest supplier
Spiciest spicer
Cool freezer
Brilliant sawer
That is my dad,
He's a butcher.

Aimee McDonnell (11)
St John the Baptist Primary School, Roscor

Market Day

Doors were unlocked
Whilst shelves were restocked
Dirt was lifted
While dust was shifted
People gathered
Although others rathered
Just to stay at home
It was market day

Things were sold
Some out in the cold
Wind was blowing
It was really showing
It stretched from alleys
And even to valleys
It was market day.

Michelle Keenan (10)
St John the Baptist Primary School, Roscor

Hamster Kennings

Nut cruncher
Finger biter
Water drinker
Food muncher
Bar climber
Heavy sleeper
Straw digger
Pipe climber
That's my hamster
Speedy!

Aimee Freeburn (10)
St John the Baptist Primary School, Roscor

Hallowe'en

It's that time of year again
When vampires all come out of their den.

Witches on broomsticks, casting spells in the night.
Oh! They would really give you a terrible fright.

Black cats are everywhere to be seen,
Prancing, prowling, squealing, planning something very mean.

We all dress up this time of year in our very fancy gear,
Out we go to trick or treat, searching for something sweet to eat.

Colourful fireworks light up the moonlit sky,
To show the way as we pass by.

Orange pumpkins sit in silence giving light to ghosts,
Skeletons and vampires on their flight.

Rockets blasting up into the night,
They explode at a gigantic height.

Happy contented children, their laughter fills the air.
Nobody has any grudge to bear.

How I love this time of year
Just to have my friends and family near.

Serena Gallagher (10)
St John the Baptist Primary School, Roscor

Angry = Red

Anger is the colour of red chillies,
It tastes of strawberry jam,
It smells of Mum's cooking,
It sounds like sizzling water,
It feels like spongy cake.

Damien Lawn (9)
St John the Baptist Primary School, Roscor

Hallowe'en Fears!

There is a Grim Reaper at the bottom of my bed,
Every night he tickles my toes!
When I'm at school he sneaks downstairs
To get some food and a drink of milk.
His name is Killer.
He has dark red eyes,
Pale white skin.
At night he has me trembling in my sleep,
He tickles my toes
And nobody knows
That he is under my bed.
Killer walks about at night
And gives me a fright!
But in my own way,
I'd miss him if he went away!

Jenny Campbell (10)
St John the Baptist Primary School, Roscor

The Crocodile

The crocodile so horrid and vile,
The crocodile with the wicked smile.

The crocodile with his scaly skin,
He has committed every sin.

The crocodile with his teeth so white,
If you aren't careful he'll give you a bite.

The crocodile he is so mean,
The crocodile with his skin so green.

The crocodile makes everyone scared,
Well I don't know for sure it's just what I've heard.

The crocodile so horrid and vile,
The crocodile with the wicked smile.

Ryan Gormley (11)
St John the Baptist Primary School, Roscor

Erne Gaels

I joined a team in yellow and black
Just for a bit of crack
They are called Erne Gaels
And we are as hard as nails!

We are from a wee village called Belleek
But we also have players from Mulleek
We are cool
But we are no fools!

Rain, hail or snow
We can put on a good show
We are proud to wear the yellow and black
Our aim is to win the cup back.

Eddie and Brendan train the team
And we play like a dream
Eddie says, 'Give it more spark
Or we will be in the dark!'
Brendan says, 'Come on or
We will never make it to Croke Park!'

Cáolan Travers (10)
St John the Baptist Primary School, Roscor

Nothing To Do?

Nothing to do?
Nothing to do?
Flush your pet hamster down the loo!
Nothing to do?
Nothing to do?
Fling elephant poo at the zoo!
Nothing to do?
Nothing to do?
Jump off your house and say *wahoo!*

Conor Gormley (9)
St John the Baptist Primary School, Roscor

Love

Love is as red as bright red flowers
It is the taste of bright strawberries
It smells like a big blueberry
It sounds of children roaring in the background
It feels like being wrapped up in my bed all cosy
And warm on a cold winter's day.

Philip Denning (10)
St John the Baptist Primary School, Roscor

Love

Love is as red as strawberries.
It tastes of chilli sauce.
It smells of a burning fire
And it sounds like lots of sparkles
And it feels so chilli and spicy like sauce.

Catherine Shaw (10)
St John the Baptist Primary School, Roscor

Fearful Forest

Trembling with fear, horror and terror
In the planet of injurious predators.

All day long you hear and smell
Ghastly creatures destroy their prey.

In the forest these ghastly creatures
Are drifting in their little black cloaks!

They suck human's blood, eat pig's guts
And licks the brain of a unicorn.

Brendan Haveron (10)
St Mary's Primary School, Maghery

A Smile

Smiling is cool
You can catch it like the flu
When someone smiled at me today
I started smiling too.

When I went to the shop today
I went to a man in blue
I smiled at him and suddenly I realised
He started smiling too.

That man in blue he had the flu
So he went to the local chemist
He looked at a girl who wasn't well
He smiled and then she smiled too.

Ben Crealey (10)
St Mary's Primary School, Maghery

Fear

A werewolf came out today
To catch its prey
In a frightful way.

The dripping blood
Came from his gob
It was so disgusting
It needed a rub.

He ripped and tore
Till his gums were sore
It was so tasty
He wanted some more.

After his feed he ran at speed
To get his next victim
By trying to trick him!

Neil McConville (9)
St Mary's Primary School, Maghery

Wintertime

Winter comes once a year
Every day it comes near
Throwing snowballs at your friends
Slipping and sliding on the ice
You wish it would never end.

Cold winter mornings
Mr Jack Frost biting our fingers and toes
Frost on the fields and roads
Icicles hanging from trees
Everywhere as cold as ice.

Wearing our hats and coats
Stamping our feet, rubbing our hands
I think we should go inside
To sit by the blazing fire
Wintertime we all enjoy.

Children look forward to Christmas
Christmas decorations shiny and bright
Oh such excitement
Opening presents and celebrations
The highlight of winter.

Roisin McConville (10)
St Mary's Primary School, Maghery

Summer

Summer is a time to play
You can run and jump
In every way

Summer is a time for fun
You can skip around
And dance and run

Summer is just the best
But at the end
You need a rest!

Lee McConville (9)
St Mary's Primary School, Maghery

Mr Gook My Teacher

Mr Gook my teacher
He is very smart.
He teaches many things,
Like about the human heart.
Maths, science, English and history,
A lot of it is still a mystery.

On Tuesday we go to the pool,
Yippee! We get out of school.

He loves music and plays the guitar;
If he goes on X-Factor
Maybe Simon will make him a star.

Emmet McParland (10)
St Mary's Primary School, Maghery

Holiday

Get out your suitcase,
Pack all your toys.
It's time to get ready,
To make some noise.

Get in the car
And off you go,
Off to the ship dock,
Row, row, row.

Or you can always go by plane,
It gets a bit bumpy on the runway lane.
So close your eyes and hold on tight,
We're going on an EasyJet flight.

Shannon Tennyson (11)
St Mary's Primary School, Maghery

The Singing Competition

I've practised now for three weeks,
It kind of gives me the creepy freaks.

I'm filled with fears,
Cries and tears.
Help me someone
So I can be number one.

When I'm up there
People start to stare;
When I sing
People start to care.

I have finished now
And I love the crowd.
They all think
I need a drink.

Coleen Cushnahan (10)
St Mary's Primary School, Maghery

The Cat And The Mouse

Off I went along the green fields
Searching for a field mouse you see.
I walked and walked for miles that day,
I guess I travelled a long, long way.

I was feeling rather tired, about to head home.
Then with a glance of an eye I spied one.
I chased it over hills and into the town.
Women were screaming and running around.
Children were squealing, as loud as they could,
My day turned out to be so good.

Eoin Tennyson (9)
St Mary's Primary School, Maghery

Winter

Winter is the best season to play
Making snowmen every day,
Watching the snowflakes falling down.
Elves telling Santa it's time now;
Delivering the presents
To us children who are good,
Waiting are those in a bad mood.

Reindeer swooping down from the sky,
Santa watching from the corner of his eye,
Everyone throwing snowy snowballs at each other,
Lucky for us it didn't hit another.

Eimhear Cushnahan (10)
St Mary's Primary School, Maghery

The Sea

The sea is nice and long
It is like a joyous song.
It can be weak,
It can be strong
And sometimes it's quite wrong.

Sometimes it's big,
Sometimes it's wee,
Sometimes dangerous,
Not like a flea.

It can be kind,
It can be tough
And sometimes very rough;
Who'd be a fish!

Conor Devlin (9)
St Mary's Primary School, Maghery

Winter

Winter is the king of snowmen,
Turning apples into snowballs,
Cold but fun we like to throw
Causing mayhem in the snow.
Snowflakes glisten on the frozen pavement
Like shining crystals in the moonlight.

The snow is white
Like a polar bear's furry white coat.
Outside we wear our coats
But inside fires burn brightly
To keep the family warm.
Round the fire with mugs of chocolate,
Snug and warm we watch
As winter dances around.

Winter comes for a short three months,
Enjoy it while it lasts.
Make the most before it's out,
Ski or hike
Choose what you like.

Tiarnan Branagh (9)
St Mary's Primary School, Maghery

The Dragon Boy

There was a boy
Who was a dragon
He breathed out flames
Of red-hot fire.
His mum and dad used him
To light the fire.
He saved people from beasts
And people gave him feasts.
He is called the Dragon King.

Paul Devine (10)
St Mary's Primary School, Maghery

The Haunted House

They say that house is haunted,
They say it's full of beasts.
Tonight is Hallowe'en,
The night they have their feast.

My friends and I are playing trick or treat,
Along the haunted road.
But we dare not to go in the haunted house,
In case we get turned into a toad.

It has dark windows and dark walls
And a path leading up to the door.
But no one goes inside there,
It has never happened before.

We see the little windows,
With shadows floating about.
We shall not enter the haunted house
And that is sure without doubt.

Orlaith Robinson (10)
St Mary's Primary School, Maghery

Death

Death is like a cracked bottle of red wine,
People die all the time.
Some death is slow,
Some death is quick,
Some death is painful,
But everyone's eyes will flick (closed).

Death can be caused by cancer or flame,
Some death is full of blood and pain.
But everyone dies eventually
So when you're in Heaven,
You'll see me.

Iarlaith Hendron (10)
St Mary's Primary School, Maghery

Cardiff City Poem

Come on the City
They are the team for me.

Robbie Fowler is the best
Better than all the rest.
Floyd Hasselbaink scoring again
Causing their goalkeeper a lot of pain.

Come on the City
They are the team for me.

Parry and Ledley on the wing
Look at them dart and also spin.
Purse scoring a pen
Their keeper exclaimed, 'Not again!'

Come on the City
They are the team for me.

McPhail shooting with all his might
His shot on goal swerves in on the right.
The Grange End let out a cheer
Next year it's the Premiership here!

Lee Thomas (9)
St Nicholas' CW Primary School, Cardiff

The Football Match

Get up lazily, brushing teeth carelessly,
Get dressed sloppily, brush hair sleepily
Before I go to the match.

Dribbling skillfully, shooting aimfullly,
Team scoring rapidly, goalie diving helplessly
At the first half.

Manager happy, other team scoring!
Scoring the winner! Winning the cup!
At the second half.

Luke Williams (9)
St Nicholas' CW Primary School, Cardiff

Love And Hate

Love
Love is red like red roses blooming in the ground.
It feels like a happy feeling coming from someone.
It tastes like chocolate melting in your mouth.
It looks like flowers growing taller and taller.
It sounds like sweet music coming from the birds.
It smells like fresh daffodils.

Hate
Hate is black like a stormy night.
It feels like stabbing forks sticking into you.
It tastes like running blood dripping from arms.
It looks like a devil appearing in your face.
It sounds like an electric shock in your body.
It smells like an old cabbage rotting in a rubbish bin.
Hate is where you will lose everything.

Taylor Rees Maher (10)
St Nicholas' CW Primary School, Cardiff

Light And Dark

Light is a diamond sparkling all night long,
Dark is a fear when the clock goes dong.

Light is a twinkle from the stars high above,
Dark is a nightmare when there's no more love.

Light is like a diva dancing until dawn breaks,
Dark is like a charging rhino causing an earthquake.

Light is as bright as the shiny sun,
Dark is a black cave and not much fun.

Light is a flash of lightning shooting from the sky,
Dark as the blitz planes dropping bombs as they fly.

Emily Kathryn Azzopardi (9)
St Nicholas' CW Primary School, Cardiff

The Party

Wake up excitedly, having a bath peacefully,
Get dressed quickly,
Get Mum to drive me there fast.
Before the party.

Arrive there excited,
Playing games playfully,
Karaoke with my friends loudly
At the party.

Go home tiredly,
Eating my party gifts with my brother calmly,
Having a snack then going to bed tiredly.
After the party.

Hannah Jane Clarke (9)
St Nicholas' CW Primary School, Cardiff

The Holiday

Get your bags packed
Get food quickly, get your bags happily,
Start to travel excitedly, have a snack hungrily.

Got to the hotel
Unpacking bags very fast, happily looking around,
Slowly eating dinner, get to bed tiredly.

Journey home
Pack your bags sadly, get everything in the car drowsily,
Get home sleepily, get carried thankfully to bed.

Lukas Wallis (8)
St Nicholas' CW Primary School, Cardiff

A Girl Called . . .

There was a girl called Paige
Who once sang on a stage.
She sang so loud she killed the crowd
So they locked her up in a cage.

There was a girl called Shellie
Who loved to watch the telly.
Her eyes fell out
So she gave a big shout
But then she went back to watching the telly.

There was a girl called Hannah
Who ate a huge banana.
She turned to a monkey
And said, 'That was funky!'
Then had a dance with a spanner.

Paige Williams (10)
St Nicholas' CW Primary School, Cardiff

The Fête

Get up tired, get dressed slowly,
Brush my teeth quickly, get my bag before the fête.

Having good fun on the rides,
Having a really happy time,
Having very fluffy candyfloss,
Having a fun time on the bouncy castle at the fête.

Have a bath, wash my hair,
Get dried, put my PJs on,
Go to bed sweetly after the fête.

Chloe Newman (8)
St Nicholas' CW Primary School, Cardiff

Simpsons' Pancakes

Ingredients
100ozs of Homer
50g of Bart skateboarding
70ozs of Lisa
90kgs of Marge
A sprinkle of laughter
A spoonful of dohs
50 cots filled with Maggie

Method
Put in 50g of Bart skateboarding.
Sprinkle the 50 cots full of Maggie and mix.
Add 100ozs of Homer and 70g of Lisa and beat with a fork.
(Doh)n't worry if the mixture doh, doh, dohs.
Mix in 90kgs of Marge and a sprinkle of laughter.
But don't forget to grate your dohs over the mixture
And fry at 220°F.
To sweeten it add lemon and sugar.
Serve up and enjoy with your family and friends.

Emily Ann Thomas (10)
St Nicholas' CW Primary School, Cardiff

Dolphin, Dolphin

Dolphin, dolphin leaping high,
Across the world and across the sky.
Splashing through the stormy sea,
As it stared straight at me.

Dolphin, dolphin stretching high.
Dolphin, dolphin do not lie.
Dolphin, dolphin touch your nose.
Dolphin, dolphin touch my toes.

Dolphin, dolphin in a fix.
Dolphin, dolphin doing tricks,
Swimming in the enormous pool.
Dolphin, dolphin you're so cool.

Rachel Maria Jones (10)
St Nicholas' CW Primary School, Cardiff

Evil/Love

Evil is red like an angry devil
It feels like a devil laughing in my ear
It tastes like blood shooting from your toe
It smells like smelly shoes which are a thousand years old
It looks like an ugly monster who looks like a devil
It sounds like the music of rock!
Evil always reminds me of Hell!

Love is red like a big heart
It feels like a big squishy cushion
It tastes like marshmallows in my mouth
It looks like cute bears hugging
It sounds like bluebirds singing
It smells like perfume on a woman
Love always reminds me of candles.

Nathan Stephens (10)
St Nicholas' CW Primary School, Cardiff

Acrostic Hamilton

L ewis Hamilton as he wins.
E ventually Alonso spins, yes.
W here Hamilton thinks Ron Dennis is king.
I mola is an easy track for him to win.
S chumacher's not a patch on him.

H igh up the ranking as he is.
A s Lewis gets another championship win.
M aybe he'll stay, maybe not.
I think getting girls is no problem Lewis.
L eader of the championship he is.
T he best rookie you have ever seen.
O n McLaren's motoring team.
N ico Rosberg is nothing compared to him.

Thomas Harvey (9)
St Nicholas' CW Primary School, Cardiff

Love And Anger

Love is red like beautiful roses.
Love feels like chocolate running down my chin.
Love tastes like fluffy soft clouds in the sky.
Love looks like my heart pounding.
Love sounds like someone calling my name gently.
Love smells like scented flowers.
Love reminds me of two people kissing in the park.

Anger is black like the dark dull night.
Anger feels like nails scratching my back.
Anger tastes like mouldy milk.
Anger looks like starving children in Africa.
Anger smells like green gone off cheese from two years ago.
Anger reminds me of nothing nice at all.

Chloe Bridgeman (10)
St Nicholas' CW Primary School, Cardiff

The Blitz

Hi Ted and hi Ned,
How come Meg Henry is next door?
Angry people shouting so loud,
The air raid and searchlights shining so high.

Air raid sirens going off
Soldiers saying, 'Goodbye mate!'
One of them running down the street,
With a gas mask over his face.

The other side of London,
Big Ben pointing at 12 o'clock, all houses covered.
The bombs blowing the houses down,
Poor old Hitler is underground.

Michael Foley (11)
St Nicholas' CW Primary School, Cardiff

My Box Of Dreams

My box of dreams
A stained shimmering glass box.
It appears to be empty.
My box of dreams
Kept in a black corner in my mind.
When I open it I see
A golden flickering light.
I see me dancing in the middle.
My dream is to fly away
And come back another day.
I wish I could be a famous dancer
And meet Victoria Beckham.
I hope my dreams come true.
If not,
They are safe
Tucked away in my mind forever.

Chantelle Morgan (10)
Ysgol Cynlais, Swansea

My Box Of Dreams

My box is lovely and shiny
A glamorous, golden magical box
Shooting stars fly out
My dreams hang on
To the shooting stars
To move to live in the sun
To be a famous singer
To swim with the dolphins
To stop pollution
My shooting stars fly back in
I'll tell you about them tomorrow.

Clarice Critchley (10)
Ysgol Cynlais, Swansea

My Box Of Dreams

On my box of dreams
There are gold glittery stars,
Red shimmering hearts
And multicoloured swirly patterns,
My box of dreams.

My box of dreams
Opens when I have drifted off to sleep,
All wonderful things come out,
It's magical,
My box of dreams.

What comes out of my box of dreams?
Party poppers and streamers,
Rainbows and glitter,
Birds and animals,
My box of dreams.

In my box of dreams
I have special memories,
Secrets,
Thoughts,
My box of dreams.

The most important thing
In my box of dreams,
Is the wonderful, wonderful
Dreams.

Stacey Griffin (10)
Ysgol Cynlais, Swansea

Autumn

A utumn is a time to celebrate.
U nder all the brown crispy leaves animals hide.
T he trees' leaves are falling on the floor.
U p on trees the nests are there.
M y birthday is in the beginning of autumn.
N uts are on the floor.

Siân Poynton (8)
Ysgol Cynlais, Swansea

My Box Of Dreams

My box of dreams,
Greeny-blue with sparkles,
It opens up at night with a water fountain popping up,
In the water there's footie stars,
Glitters flying around,
There's lights shining up the room,
It's got Kraze magazines inside.

My box of dreams,
It's kept in the back of the wardrobe,
I press a button and Match magazines float out to me,
It shoots out posters of footie stars,
Ronaldo and Rooney always come to life,
It can fly on a magic carpet around the room,
It has a genie lamp underneath.

My box of dreams,
It's full up to the brim,
It's wooden but as powerful as Hercules or even the sun,
There is an emergency spy kit inside,
There is an angel and a devil inside or even outside on the shelf,
That's my box of dreams.

Daniel Smith (10)
Ysgol Cynlais, Swansea

Warrior

W eapons getting ready for a long battling day.
A ttacking their enemies the Romans.
R oaring and running down to win their fight,
R ipping throats and bodies killed, lying down on the battlefield.
I ron swords clashing through the air.
O nly the Celts are living now,
R ush to the roundhouses, what shall we do next?

Naiomi Williams (8)
Ysgol Cynlais, Swansea

My Special Friend

Long straight blonde hair,
Emerald-green eyes,
Loves eating margarita pizzas,
Absolutely hates Brussels sprouts,
Likes doing monkey faces,
Excellent at the splits,
Kind and generous.

Good at horse riding,
Two months older than me,
Very funny,
Loves Hannah Montana,
Very clever,
Her favourite subject is PE,
Always there for me,
Has one dog called Suki.

Faye Lewis (9)
Ysgol Cynlais, Swansea

My Special Brother

Short brown hair,
Really blue eyes like the sky,
His favourite hobby is football,
Very kind,
Favourite food is pizza,
Hates baked beans.

Good at maths,
When he goes he buys me sweets,
Likes baking Welsh cakes,
He likes his computer,
His smile is nice,
He's my favourite person.

Luc Caines (9)
Ysgol Cynlais, Swansea

My Uncle

He has dark chocolate-brown eyes,
Takes me everywhere,
He is very funny with me,
His favourite hobby is going up to his shed and doing weights,
He is kind and helpful,
He is 18 years old,
He has short black hair.

He really likes his food
And he likes to go out with his friends,
He really hates wasps,
He likes to go to Swansea,
He is always happy,
He is really good at computers and brilliant at maths,
He buys me sweets,
Takes me to McDonald's,
His favourite colour is blue,
My uncle.

Katie Morgan (9)
Ysgol Cynlais, Swansea

My Special Person

He has eyes like brown melted chocolate,
Looks like me,
Likes making food cocktails,
Can be funny,
Likes to play the bogeyman,
He's a trampoline fan but gets knocked over a lot,
Doesn't like spiders,
Loves watching LazyTown,
I love him a lot.

David Griffiths (9)
Ysgol Cynlais, Swansea

Autumn

A ll amazing things happen in autumn.
U nder the leaves the animals are hibernating.
T hese are the colours of the leaves, red, yellow and green.
U mbrellas are scattered around Wales.
M any nuts fall from trees.
N ights get longer.

Kieran Bufton (8)
Ysgol Cynlais, Swansea

Autumn

A utumn leaves go red, green and yellow.
U nder the leaves the mice try to make themselves warm.
T he leaves fall off the trees when they are red, green and orange.
U nder the trees the hedgehogs are warm.
M y umbrellas come out when it rains.
N uts off the trees.

Dee Lewis (7)
Ysgol Cynlais, Swansea

Autumn

A ll the leaves are falling red and green.
U nder the leaves the animals sleep.
T rees have lost their leaves.
U p in the trees the brown squirrels play.
M ice hibernate under the trees.
N ights get longer.

Daisy Lovering (7)
Ysgol Cynlais, Swansea

Autumn

A utumn all animals hibernate.
U nder the red, yellow and green leaves animals hibernate.
T rees are losing their leaves.
U nder the trees moles are hibernating.
M ice are hibernating in their houses.
N ests up high in the treetops.

Luke Smith (8)
Ysgol Cynlais, Swansea

My Box Of Dreams

My box is by my bed,
When I open it
Shooting stars
And glittering sparkling dust
Come towards me,
Hypnotises me.
My dream
To save the world
Disappears for another day.

Joshua Taylor (10)
Ysgol Cynlais, Swansea

Autumn

A utumn leaves change to red and brown.
U nder the crispy golden leaves animals hide.
T he crunchy leaves are fun to play in.
U mbrellas are going up in the rain.
M y birthday is in autumn.
N ow the animals are hibernating.

Laura Harper (7)
Ysgol Cynlais, Swansea

My Box Of Dreams

My box of dreams
In a secret place
Under my soft cuddly bed
Carefully covered with sparkling shooting stars
Only I can see my mystery box
My wonderful box is a magical blue
Securely locked it is extraordinary
My box is a small cube

When I open my unusual box
There is a great whoosh
And then a massive bang
My heart beat faster
I see a dazzling shiny star
When I open my box

I am sucked into my dream
Everything is different
I land with a huge bump
No one is fighting
Everyone is happy
I also jump
I am able to fly
Into the high sky

Then I land with a big bang
And I am transported back home
I leave my lovely box
For another day.

Kathryn Potter (10)
Ysgol Cynlais, Swansea

My Box Of Dreams

A sparkling, dazzling silver box,
A shining star on the front,
A window,
Hidden under my bed,
I open my secret box,
I see shooting stars
Zooming into the sky,
My dreams are . . .
To be a famous poet,
To be the fastest runner in the world,
For the world to be a better place.
When I close the box
Glitter falls from the sky
Ready for another day.

Megan Robini (10)
Ysgol Cynlais, Swansea

My Box Of Dreams

A purple box
With shooting stars,
When you open it
My dream appears,
A special medicine
To cure diabetes
For life,
I close my box,
My dreams are there forever.

Ffion Griffiths (10)
Ysgol Cynlais, Swansea

My Box Of Dreams

My box of dreams
Is a golden cube
With silver writing saying my dreams,
It is a magical box
With colourful gleaming ribbons.
My box is under my bed secretly hidden
And it's locked with a shiny blue key.

When I open my box of dreams
I see multicoloured mists
Hypnotising me.
I feel as if I'm in another world.

Now front row seats of the Millennium Stadium
Meeting the Welsh players,
Roars and bangs in the crowd,
Wales are winning 28-7 against New Zealand.

I have a dream there's no more wars,
No more weapons
And to live in a peaceful environment.

Then when I close it . . .
I fall back on my bed,
The box rattling and shaking,
Then silent.

My box of dreams for another day.

Elliot Antcliff (10)
Ysgol Cynlais, Swansea

Warrior

W ar is coming, weapons ready for battle.

A rmoured Celts waiting for a call.

R oundhouses empty, hill fort gates open, everyone at war.

R uthless Romans stand with heavy shields.

I ron swords clashing, shields bashing, spears flying everywhere.

O n the battleground bodies dead and tired.

R etreating warriors limping to their hill fort.

Finley Topping (8)
Ysgol Cynlais, Swansea

My Box Of Dreams

A shiny mysterious golden box
Easy to open
A gleaming silver lock
A short key
Hidden under my dark bed
When I open my box
Sparkling shooting stars
Fill the air
My dreams are
No bombs
No floods
My future
To be a successful teacher
I close my box
Shooting stars sucked back
I lock it
Ready for another day.

Emily Stringer (10)
Ysgol Cynlais, Swansea

My Box Of Dreams

My box of dreams
Is multicoloured, dazzling,
A shiny and mysterious box,
It is translucent
And rectangular.

My box of dreams
Is in a secret place
Where no one knows.

My box of dreams,
I open the box
And shooting stars with coloured
Dazzling diamonds come out
And grey mystical mist
With exploding fireworks.

My dreams are to swim
In the clear blue water
With the sparkling friendly dolphins
And to have a peaceful life.

When I close the box
The exploding fireworks
Get sucked in with
My dreams at the end.

Sophie Thomas (10)
Ysgol Cynlais, Swansea

My Box Of Dreams

My box of dreams
Is magical, mysterious and colourful,
Silver gold and glittering red,
Stained glass,
It shines in the sun's golden rays.

My box of dreams
Is hidden under my bed.

My box of dreams
Is opened by a shiny silvery glowing key,
I open it . . .
Out comes grey magical mist,
Dull and very smoky.

My dream is . . .
To run on to the pitch,
That belongs to the theatre of dreams,
Score a goal,
In the game that wins
The Premiership.

My box of dreams
Sucks in the swirling mist
And all goes dark,
Nothing! Blackness!
All for another night.

Callum Close (10)
Ysgol Cynlais, Swansea

My Box Of Dreams

My box of dreams,
An ancient wooden box
In a mystical chest,
When I open it
A grey mist appears,
When I am in the box
I am a brave paratrooper
Ready for action,
Holding the rugby World Cup
Wearing my Scottish jersey,
A peaceful world,
No litter,
Lots of happy children,
Lambs prancing in the field,
Then
I am sucked back
Into the present
Ready for another day.

Fraser Topping (10)
Ysgol Cynlais, Swansea

My Pet Snake

My pet snake it's long and thin,
All my mam wants is to put him in the bin!
His name is Scooby Dooby Doo
And oh, how I'd like him to meet you.
He lives in a tank that's not very big,
Among some wood pieces he likes to dig.
He goes round and round until he's in a coil.
We switch on his heat pad and he likes to boil.
He eats mice and thinks they are delicious
And when he slides and slithers, oh how he looks suspicious.
My pet snake makes me smile,
Oh I hope I have him for a long while.

Owain Lewis (8)
Ysgol Gymraeg Bro Ogwr, Brackida

Lonely

Looks like you're about to cry
With icy breath going down your spine
Nothing to hold in your cold hands
No hope in your heart
No life in your body
Nothing to comfort you when you're sad
Feels like you are going mad
Nothing to do, nothing to say
Everything is getting in your way
It feels like someone has laid a brick on your back.

Lewis Robertson (11)
Ysgol Yr Esgob, Caerwys

Lewis

L azy
E xcellent
W eird
I nteresting
S illy.

Tomos Eden (11)
Ysgol Yr Esgob, Caerwys

Lewis

L augh
E xtreme
W eird
I ncredible
S illy.

Jack Read (10)
Ysgol Yr Esgob, Caerwys

Disneyland Florida

Such a sight I saw:

Popcorn stands and Tinkerbell sequins
And rides like Splash Mountain.
Mickey Mouse and Minnie Mouse signing autographs
And lots of other things like fireworks above the castle.

Such food I tasted:

Chilli chips and cheese
And toasted waffles with slimy maple syrup,
Funnel cakes and pizza with Coke.

Such a smell I smelt:

Toffee popcorn and fresh air
And burning from the fireworks.

Such a sound I heard:
Jiminy Cricket speaking to you
And people speaking about how lovely the place is.

Such things I felt:

Wet carriages from the wet rides
And the soft bricks of the castle.

Disneyland, Florida.

Jessikah Falshaw (10)
Ysgol Yr Esgob, Caerwys

A Poem About My Senses

Such a sound I heard:
My dad's in the milking parlour, milking the cows,
Cows bellowing in the yard
And dogs barking at them,
Such a sound I heard.

Such a sight I saw:
Sitting next to my bedroom window I watched
The horse running round the field,
My dad on the tractor cutting the hedges,
Such a sight I saw.

Such a taste I tasted:
My mum's delicious jam so tasty,
Drop scones are so tasty you will love them
And they make your mouth water,
Such a taste I tasted.

Such a smell I smelt:
The smell of green fields as my dad is harvesting
And the smell of corn
As the combine harvester blew the corn into the trailer,
Such a smell I smelt.

Michael Evans (9)
Ysgol Yr Esgob, Caerwys

Young Writers Information

We hope you have enjoyed reading this book - and that you will continue to enjoy it in the coming years.

If you like reading and writing poetry drop us a line, or give us a call, and we'll send you a free information pack.

Alternatively if you would like to order further copies of this book or any of our other titles, then please give us a call or log onto our website at www.youngwriters.co.uk

**Young Writers Information
Remus House
Coltsfoot Drive
Peterborough
PE2 9JX**

(01733) 890066